The Sinking of the USS *Cairo*

The Sinking of the USS *Cairo*

John C. Wideman

UNIVERSITY PRESS OF MISSISSIPPI
JACKSON

Manufactured in the United States of America

96 95 94 93 4 3 2 1

First edition

The paper in this book meets the guidelines for permanence and durability of the Committee on Production Guidelines for Book Longevity of the Council on Library Resources.

Library of Congress Cataloging-in-Publication Data

Wideman, John C.
The sinking of the USS Cairo / John C. Wideman.
p. cm.
Includes bibliographical references and index.
ISBN 0-87805-617-3
1. Cairo (Gunboat) 2. Torpedo-boats—Confederate States of America. I. Title.
E595.C3W53 1993
973.7'57—dc20 92-39651
CIP

British Library Cataloging-in-Publication data available

This book is dedicated to all the men and women of the Confederate States intelligence services, whether called torpedo corps, secret service, scout, or spy. They devoted themselves to their crafts of espionage, sabotage, and subversion, going behind enemy lines and entering the enemy's heartland in disguise, alone, unafraid, and sometimes unarmed, without the succor and support of comrades in arms, knowing that at any moment their capture would result in a spy's death from the gallows or the firing squad.

> "There will always be espionage. . . . And, there will always be men who, from love of adventure or a sense of duty, will risk shameful death to secure information valuable to their country."
>
> Somerset Maugham
> Preface to the American Edition of *Ashenden*

And, of course, to Zere McDaniel (1821–1870).

Contents

Introduction

The USS *Cairo* is the only surviving example of a Civil War–era Union ironclad gunboat. It survived because it was destroyed. Sunk by a Confederate torpedo in 1862, it languished in the mud of the Yazoo River for more than a century. Although its location was known to local residents, it was "rediscovered" and raised in the mid-1960s. It is now a premier exhibit at the Vicksburg National Military Park, Vicksburg, Mississippi.

In 1862 the use of torpedoes to protect harbors and deny the enemy access to certain watercourses was a controversial issue. The use of time bombs and land mines was considered a violation of the rules of war. The story of the sinking of the USS *Cairo* is a part of that controversy.

There is a controversy over who invented the torpedo that sank the *Cairo*. Zere McDaniel (with a colleague, Francis Ewing) and Thomas Weldon each claimed to have discovered the friction primer in making the torpedo that sank the *Cairo*. The claims were made in hopes of receiving a large bounty offered by the Confederate government in a secret act to encourage such operations. To support these claims, statements under oath were taken from almost every man involved.

There is a modern controversy over how the torpedo that sank the *Cairo* was detonated. David D. Porter's statement that the torpedo was "evidently fired by a galvanic battery" has been accepted by historians and repeated in the telling of the story of the *Cairo*. Porter, however, relied on secondhand information from naval personnel who had virtually no understanding of torpedoes. The facts that unfold in this book tell an entirely different tale of how the torpedo was made and exploded. These facts destroy the previously held theories concerning construction of the torpedo. The torpedo that sank the *Cairo* was not electrically fired but was fired with artillery friction primers set off when a boat disturbed a trigger lanyard.

My research uncovered previously unreported primary sources, identifying for the first time the Confederate naval personnel who built the torpedoes on the Yazoo River in December 1862 and how they did it. Affidavits and letters of these participants, used to support the claims of McDaniel and Weldon and stored in the National Archives for almost 130 years, describe how the torpedo was constructed. They also describe in detail Confederate activities on the day the *Cairo* was sunk and for several days before and after.

The story of the *Cairo* must include praise for historian Edwin C. Bearss, who, with a band of stalwart companions, raised the *Cairo* from its mucky grave in the Yazoo River so it might be enjoyed by generations of Americans to come. The *Cairo* now sits in its own museum space at the Vicksburg National Military Park. To complete the story, one should visit the *Cairo*, walk its decks, and inspect the hole that the Confederate torpedo tore in her port side hull that fateful day in 1862.

Unconventional Confederate warfare operations have not been written about in a detailed, comprehensive manner. The seminal work on Confederate torpedo operations is Milton Perry's *Infernal Machines: The Story of Confederate Submarine and Mine Warfare*, published in 1965. Since then, the history of this type of warfare has been relegated to the occasional article or brief mention in other publications. William Tidwell and his associates touched on the subject in their work, *Come Retribution: The Confederate Secret Service and the Assassination of Abraham Lincoln*. Several other authors told a bit about what the Confederate naval personnel did on December 12, 1862, the day they sank the *Cairo*. No one has gone to the core of the Confederate torpedo operations, which resulted in the sinking of the *Cairo*.

Integral to this story is Zere McDaniel, a Confederate officer. His part in the destruction of the USS *Cairo* has been reconstructed from official government sources and contemporary historical records. Additionally, the story covers McDaniel's life as a special operations officer in the Confederate secret service. McDaniel's secret service operations (sabotage and behind-the-lines operations with unconventional forces) were similar to those that today are performed by United States military special operations units such as Army Special Forces, Navy SEALs, or Marine Recon units.

The chapters concerning McDaniel's special operations and the formation of his secret service company add to the knowledge of several well-known operations and give further foundation to the history of military intelligence and military special operations during the Civil War. McDaniel was a prolific letter writer, particularly when he had to justify his actions to superiors or when he thought he was being wronged. His detailed writings, and those of his contemporaries, give us further insight into Confederate secret service operations and identify some of the participants in these operations. Professional intelligence officers who read this book will take some comfort in knowing that the bureaucratic problems they faced in the second half of the twentieth century were suffered by their predecessors in the nineteenth century.

In every war, there are mechanical geniuses such as those who developed the atom bomb, jet propulsion, and airborne warfare in World War II and the tank, the airplane, and poison gas in World War I. In the Civil War, warfare was changed radically with the invention of more violent ways to kill. The Civil War saw the transition from cap and ball to metallic cartridge; from single-shot rifles to repeating weapons, including the predecessor of the machine gun; from European fixed-mass warfare to the mobile, fluid, multisite battlefields that dominate warfare to this day.

Zere McDaniel was an aggressive, inventive Southern renaissance man. He patented one invention in 1860 and two others during the war. Controversy, mystery, rumor, and legend surround Zere McDaniel, the sinking of the *Cairo*, and his special operations. I have presented all of that as I found it. All of the research materials found on Zere McDaniel were either written contemporaneously during the war or within the living memory of the participants. Historians are fortunate that many Confederate records survived the pillage of Richmond. Oddly enough, the survival of those records owes much to the assassination of Abraham Lincoln and the conspiracy perceived by the U.S. government.

Zere McDaniel's name is probably a derivative of the biblical name Zerah (also Zara, Zarah) found in Genesis, Numbers, Joshua, and First and Second Chronicles. The translation from Hebrew is "dawning." In various documents associated with him, his name is spelled Zere, Zera, Zeary, Ziri, Ziry, Zeri, initial Z only, and Zedekiah. The name Zedekiah is used rarely, never by McDaniel himself, and almost exclusively in the claim-related documents and a couple of government sources. It was apparently supplied by a well-meaning attorney or a politician. It has been repeated by historians who did not have access to or do the research to determine his real name. In legal documents he always signed his name "Z. McDaniel" or "Zere McDaniel." For simplicity I have chosen to use Zere throughout this book except when variations appear in direct quotes.

I owe the completion of this book to family members, archivists, friends, correspondents, and historians, some of whom I would like to thank here: E. Dixon Ericson, my mentor, close friend, and most severe critic; M. Timothy Koontz, who provided me with a quiet place to write this book; Perry Bryant, an amateur historian of Glasgow, Kentucky, who opened the vault in the records room of the Barren County, Kentucky, Courthouse to me; the staffs of the National Archives; the Library of Congress; the Mississippi Department of Archives and History, Archives and Library Division; the Alabama Department of Archives and History; the Louisiana State Library, Reference Division; the Virginia State Library Archives Division; the Kentucky State Department of Libraries and Archives; and the West Virginia Department of Culture and History, Archives Division, without whom this research would have been impossible; Kenneth Slack, bibliographer of the Blake Library of Confederate History at the Morrow Library, Marshall University, Huntington, West Virginia; Chet and Thelma Wideman, my father and mother, who gave me the intellectual freedom to be me; Emmy McDaniel Wideman, Marguerite Wideman Altman, and the other family members who have contributed through the years; Roberta Ward Alexander, one of the finest "steel magnolias," who reaffirmed my "southernness"; the staff at the Vicksburg National Military Park, particularly Terry Winschel and Val Cooper; Gordon Cotton of the Vicksburg Old Courthouse Museum, who provided moral support, encouragement, and some key leads; Katherine Henderson, who kept the English in order; Lesa Smith, on whose portable laptop computer most of this book originally was written; and last but not least, my wife, Charlene, who has more in common with Elizabeth Berry McDaniel than she realizes.

Special recognition is due Seetha A-Srinivasan and her staff at the University Press of Mississippi for recognizing the value of my early submissions and to Trudie Calvert, the copyeditor, for breathing life into them.

The Sinking of the USS *Cairo*

1

Constantly Engaged in the Cause

January 1862–October 1862

In July 1863, Zere McDaniel wrote Jefferson Davis, president of the Confederate States of America: "I am forty-two years old, a native and a citizen of the state of Kentucky, before the war a mill right by profession & practice, a vocation which my skill therein rendered very lucrative, by means whereof, I was, when the war commenced, living most easily & happily with my family in Kentucky. . . . I was accumulating property which with a large debt due me I left behind when I engaged in the Confederate States. Since I left Kentucky with our Army in February 1862, I have been constantly engaged in the cause."[1]

Originally from Pittsylvania County, Virginia, Zere McDaniel came west to Barren County, Kentucky, in the late 1850s.[2] He purchased a house in Glasgow, across the street from the courthouse at the corner of Green and Washington streets,[3] where he lived with his wife, the former Elizabeth Berry, and their two infant children, Zere and Quinlinnia.

When Kentucky broke apart at the beginning of the Civil War, McDaniel, a loyal son of the South, immediately joined ranks with the Provisional Confederate Government of Kentucky. His mechanical background suited him for a new post in the government, inspector of arms, in which capacity he placed a notice in the Louisville paper:

> NOTICE: All free white males of Barren County, between the ages of eighteen and forty-five, who will not volunteer in the Confederate service, who have a gun, or guns, are required to deliver said gun or guns within twenty days, in Glasgow, Ky., at the office of the undersigned, Inspector of Arms for Barren County.
>
> All persons within the ages above named, who have taxable property to the value of $500 and upwards, who has no gun, will attend at the office aforesaid, within the time aforesaid, and make oath to the same, and pay $20 for which amount and all the guns that are delivered, said Inspector will receipt, which receipt will be evidence of debt against said Confederate Government. All persons failing to comply with this requisition will subject themselves to a fine of $50 and imprisonment until said fine is paid.
>
> The undersigned is authorized to receive, accept and qualify volunteers for the Confederate services, for the term of twelve months.
>
> Z. MC DANIEL
>
> Inspector of Arms, Barren County
>
> January 15, 1862.[4]

While McDaniel worked to support the Confederate effort in Kentucky, the strategic Union plan for prosecuting the war against the secessionist states was taking form. The Anaconda Plan, devised by the aging but brilliant General Winfield Scott, was designed to strangle the South economically and militarily through blockading eastern seaports and gaining control of the Mississippi River. President Abraham Lincoln adopted the Anaconda Plan over the protest of some of his senior military officers. Part of the plan provided for the Union navy to make a systematic reduction of Confederate strong points along the Mississippi River, ultimately gaining control of the river.

The Mississippi River served as a lifeline for the Confederacy. As long as it was open to Confederate commerce, supplies, troops, and munitions moved rapidly through the western part of the Confederate states over the miles of navigable waterways that flowed into the Mississippi River and through Mississippi, Kentucky, Tennessee, Louisiana, Arkansas, Missouri, and Alabama. From the confluence of the Mississippi and Ohio rivers at Cairo, Illinois, south to Memphis, Tennessee, the eastern edge of the Mississippi River is commanded at most points by high bluffs. At critical points along that bluff line, Confederate forces built forts and emplaced powerful cannon. Any Union vessels attempting to travel downriver would have to run this gauntlet of forts and risk destruction.

The Mississippi River is filled with small islands, numbered consecutively beginning with Island Number 1 just below Cairo, Illinois, and continuing south to the Gulf of Mexico. One of the larger islands located in a bend of the river just south of another Confederate strong point, New Madrid, Missouri, was Island Number 10. The Confederates chose this spot to build a formidable fort.

The Union fleet began its reduction of Confederate strong points on the Mississippi in late 1861. The initial objective was to take Memphis. Beyond Memphis, the Mississippi River moves away from the bluff line and into the river plain until it reaches Vicksburg, Mississippi, the second major Union objective. Once past Memphis, Union ships had little to fear from land-based weapons until they reached Vicksburg. If they were challenged by Confederate ships, the side with superior firepower, construction, and seamanship would be the victor.

In July 1861, in hopes of achieving total naval superiority on the Mississippi River, Montgomery C. Meigs, quartermaster general of the Union Army, ordered the development and production of nine special ironclad gunboats, heavily armed, of shallow draft, and with thick armored plate. These boats would support land forces by attempting to reduce the dense artillery positions that Admiral David G. Farragut knew existed at the various Confederate strong points on the river and driving off any Confederate naval ships that might be on the scene. The heavily armored vessels could move close in to shore, near the batteries, and deliver a withering fire damaging the positions sufficiently that they could be overrun by infantry forces.

Samuel Pook designed the new ironclad gunboats, and James B. Eads built them under contract with the Union army at Carondelet (St. Louis), Missouri, and Mound City, Illinois. As each was built, it was christened with the name of a city. One ship carried the name of the city near where it was built, the USS *Cairo*. As soon as each boat was built, commissioned, and manned, it was placed into service on the river. Beginning with the launch of the keel of the *St. Louis* on October 12, 1861, gunboat keels were turned out with production-line rapidity. Within twenty days, the *Carondelet*, *Cincinnati*, *Louisville*, *Mound City*, *Cairo*, and *Pittsburg* were laid. Eads took the hull of a former snag boat, the *Benton*, and made an eighth ironclad. He finished the production run with a ninth, the *Essex*. The *Benton* was used on the Mississippi River to pull up snags, underwater tree stumps, to allow safer navigation. For this purpose, it had a very powerful engine, which would enable it to pull a gunboat weighing five hundred tons or more.

The *Cairo* was a new breed of ship for a new kind of war. The wooden sailing ships that made up the United States fleet before 1861 were designed to fight in open seas against other wooden ships. Combat on inland waterways required powered vessels that could withstand close fire from land-based positions and move in shallow waters. Ironclads could also run close in and deliver a withering fire without significant concern about return fire from a wooden ship. The ironclads made a speed of about six miles per hour in still water.

A masted ship relied on the wind or a secondary internal steam engine for its movement. On inland waterways, it was a sitting target because many of the rivers and tributaries were too small to maneuver a large, masted, deep-draft ship that could move only in the center of major tributaries. The shorter, shallow-draft, self-propelled ironclads maneuvered more easily in shallow waters, particularly when fighting the current of major rivers. Finally, wooden ships could not withstand the volume and caliber of gunfire that an ironclad delivered.

Initially it was assumed that ironclads were impregnable to all but large-caliber fire. When they were constructed, torpedoes, a virtually unknown weapon, and defenses against torpedoes, were not considered. To many believers, there were no true defenses against the ironclads except other, larger, more powerfully armed ironclads. Ironclads were the transition vessels between the great wooden sailing ships of the mid-nineteenth century and the large steel combat ships of the late nineteenth century.

Military events caused the Confederate position in the West to deteriorate rapidly. By February 1862, Union forces were so strong that General Albert Sidney Johnston, commander of Confederate forces in Kentucky, was forced to withdraw into Tennessee and abandon Kentucky. Provisional Government officers, including Zere McDaniel, went with Johnston's withdrawing army because to stay invited certain retribution and imprisonment by the pro-Union government that would soon take control. McDaniel's decision was justified when the pro-Union government in Barren County indicted him for usurpation of office and treason.[5] The natural flow of march for the withdrawing Confederates was southward into Tennessee and Mississippi. McDaniel made several influential friends during his days in Kentucky, and, armed with letters of introduction from these men, he traveled to Mississippi.[6]

In Mississippi, McDaniel received an introduction to Governor John J. Pettus through the wife of George Work, a Jackson, Mississippi, attorney.[7] McDaniel related to Pettus his idea that torpedoes, or submarine batteries[8] as they were also known, placed in the waterways would wreak havoc and destruction upon Union ships and deter their movements. He sought, and apparently received, Pettus's sponsorship to work on such inventions. By May 1862, McDaniel was constructing his devices. George Work returned from the defense of Vicksburg and reported that McDaniel was at his house in May 1862, "and in a few days thereafter, I went into a room and was shown the apparatus he had prepared for the construction of torpedoes and pulleys which I saw in operation."[9]

Fort Henry (on the Tennessee River at the juncture of the river and the borders of Kentucky and Tennessee), Fort Donelson (on the Cumberland River just north of Dover, Tennessee), Columbus, Kentucky, Island Number 10, and New Madrid fell in order, although not without hard fighting. The new Union ironclad gunboats steamed into combat and were bloodied for the first time. At Fort Henry, on February 6, 1862, the USS *Essex* was shot up; several of her crew were killed and twenty-eight men scalded from a steam system rupture. At Fort Donelson, on February 13, the USS *Carondelet*, under the command of Captain Henry Walke, was hit and three of her four pilots were killed.

By May 10, 1862, the Union fleet had moved to the vicinity of Fort Pillow, forty miles north of Memphis. The reduction of Fort Pillow began with harassing fire from mortar boats. Each morning, a mortar boat tied up near Plum Point, several miles upriver from the fort, fired its rounds into the fort. An ironclad was tied up nearby to provide security for the mortar boats. On this morning, the ironclad USS *Cincinnati* had the duty of protecting the mortar boats. Confederate Fleet Captain J. Ed Montgomery arrived at Plum Point that morning with several extremely fast riverboats, which were converted to rams by adding steel supports to their bows. The *Cincinnati* cast off from her moorings and moved to engage the Confederate rams. The remaining Union fleet, which was preparing to attack Fort Pillow that day, left its moorings further upriver and moved downstream.

While the *Cincinnati* fired at the oncoming rams, one of them, the CSS

General Bragg, maneuvered behind the *Cincinnati* and struck her in the stern. Moments later, a second Confederate ram struck her in the same location, disabling her steering gear. Unable to steer or maneuver, the *Cincinnati* was helped to a nearby sandbar by a tug and her sister ironclad, the USS *Pittsburg*, where she sank in eleven feet of water. While this action was taking place, the ironclad USS *Mound City* was steaming into action. Another Confederate ram, the CSS *General Van Dorn*, rammed the *Mound City* and forced her to steam to the Arkansas shore, where she was run aground to avoid sinking in the deeper parts of the river. The other Union ironclads were brought into action piecemeal, and the Confederate rams withdrew to the protection of Fort Pillow's guns rather than risk being sunk by the ironclads' superior firepower. The *Cincinnati* and the *Mound City* were raised, repaired, and returned to service. On June 4, 1862, the Confederates, fearing envelopment by Union forces, evacuated Fort Pillow. General Pierre G. T. Beauregard's evacuation of Corinth, Mississippi, during the last week of May 1862 had placed the Memphis area in a desperate situation.

In late May 1862, McDaniel had gone north to Memphis, seeking to assist Captain J. Ed Montgomery with the defenses there. McDaniel proposed using sheet metal casings for torpedoes to be placed in the Mississippi River around Memphis. On June 5, 1862, he wired his sponsor, Governor Pettus: "Commodore Montgomery has promised to cooperate with me in the fight. See Mr. Evans to fix as many [submarine] batteries as possible. Get all the large tin buckets in the neighborhood, rip them up and have the tinner to put them in the proper shape for the powder. Work as fast as possible."[10] Colonel Charles Ellet, Jr., a Union army officer, had asked the War Department early in the war to permit him to purchase and construct steam-powered ramming ships. On March 27, 1862, the secretary of war directed Ellet to buy a number of river steamers and convert them to rams according to his own design. Within six weeks, he bought and converted seven steamers, three stern-wheel steamers, and four side-wheel steamers. He described the conversion process as follows: "Three heavy, solid timber bulkheads, from twelve to sixteen inches thick, were built, running fore and aft from stem to stern, the central one being over the keelson. These bulkheads were braced one against the other, the out ones against the hull of the boat, and all against the deck and floor timbers, thus making the whole weight of the boat add its momentum to that of the central bulkhead at the moment of collision."[11] One of Ellet's rams was the *Queen of the West*.

The Union navy, leery of the Confederate rams after the action at Plum Point in early May, sailed into the waters at Memphis with the new ram fleet, commanded by Colonel Charles Ellet, Jr., in the lead. After a short, vicious fight with the Confederate River Defence Fleet of Captain J. Ed Montgomery, in which only one Confederate ram, the *Van Dorn*, escaped during the morning hours of June 6, Memphis was surrendered to Union forces. McDaniel had not had time to effectuate his plan, and he was forced to return to Mississippi, where he went to Vicksburg to begin trials of his inventions in the rivers there.[12] Union ships now had control of the Mississippi from Cairo, Illinois, to Vicksburg, Mississippi, one of three remaining Confederate strongholds.

By July 1862, however, the Union fleet had enough experience that its command knew its ironclads were not the impregnable floating fortresses they were first believed to be. Their experiences on the upper Mississippi showed that the ironclads were vulnerable to plunging fire from elevated artillery pieces and to attacks by rams. But they had not been tested against another ironclad.

A daring Confederate naval commander, Isaac Newton Brown, rushed to complete his own ironclad, the CSS *Arkansas*, which lay at a protected naval yard at Yazoo City, Mississippi. The *Arkansas* was under construction for over a year and was moved three times to avoid capture by Union forces. It finally was brought to Yazoo City, where Brown found it when he assumed command. Brown, a twenty-seven-year veteran of the United States navy, had helped to design the *Arkansas* to be as formidable as possible. In addition to thick iron plating, he armored her prow for ramming and equipped her with rifled guns to give her weapons penetrating power.

Rear Admiral David G. Farragut learned from Confederate deserters that the Confederates were building an ironclad on the Yazoo River, but he did not believe they could build a formidable ship in such a remote place.[13] He placed his fleet, steam down to conserve valuable coal, in the Mississippi River just above Vicksburg, out of the range of Confederate shore batteries. He then ordered a reconnaissance force into the Yazoo River to search for the Confederate vessel, if it existed, and make general observations of Confederate defenses. The search force consisted of the

Eads ironclad *Carondelet* and two supporting vessels, the tinclad USS *Taylor* and the Ellet ram *Queen of the West*.

Brown, aboard the hastily completed and manned CSS *Arkansas*, decided to make a surprise run on the Union fleet. In the early morning hours of July 14, 1862, he began his move down the fifty miles of Yazoo River ahead. His plan was to arrive at Haynes' Bluff, about twenty-three miles above the mouth of the Yazoo River, around midnight and make the raid on the unsuspecting Union fleet at dawn. Brown had no intelligence about the exact location of the Union fleet.[14] His few efforts to obtain information along the route were without success. As dawn broke, Brown steamed downriver and ran into Farragut's reconnaissance force about six miles up the Yazoo River.

After an hour-long running gun battle at six miles per hour, in which the Union ships attempted a hasty withdrawal, the *Arkansas* finally steamed past the stricken *Carondelet*, dead in the water along the Yazoo bank, her hull riddled by thirteen rounds and most of her operational equipment shot away. Brown continued pursuit of the remaining Union vessels, both more lightly armored and armed but faster than the *Arkansas*.

Firing continuously at the fleeing ships, Brown entered the main channel of the Mississippi and headed downstream. The Union fleet still was lying at anchor, steam down. The first sounds to reach the fleet were confusing. Some officers thought the reconnaissance force was firing at Confederate guerrillas along the riverbanks. The last thing anyone expected was a Confederate gunboat running through the middle of the entire Union riverine fleet, but that was exactly what was happening. As Brown swept through the fleet, his gunners fired at maximum rate because there was no fear of hitting anything but an enemy vessel. The Union commanders, lacking the steam necessary for movement, could do little but take careful aim, hope to hit the *Arkansas*, and avoid hitting other Union vessels with their fire.

Brown continued his run through the fleet and landed, seriously wounded and his vessel heavily damaged, under the safety of the Confederate batteries at Vicksburg. Although the Union fleet sustained some material damage, the worst damage was to the confidence and ego of its naval commanders. Admiral Farragut wrote to Secretary of the Navy Gideon Welles, "It is with deep mortification that I announce to the department that, notwithstanding my prediction to the contrary, the iron-clad ram 'Arkansas' has at length made her appearance and taken us all by surprise."[15]

At Vicksburg, McDaniel met with several naval officers, most notably Commander Isaac Newton Brown of CSS *Arkansas* fame and the senior Confederate naval officer in the river area, and possibly Lieutenant Beverly Kennon, Jr.[16] Whether Kennon had any professional interaction with McDaniel is unknown but possible. At least one historian states that Kennon, who was experimenting with torpedoes, imparted his knowledge of them to McDaniel in the fall of 1862.[17] Contemporary records, however, indicate that McDaniel was involved with torpedoes long before the fall of 1862.[18] Richard Maury, son of Matthew Fontaine Maury, noted that after the war Kennon claimed to have been responsible for sinking the *Cairo*. Maury wrote, "Kennon claimed the credit for this but Masters McDaniel and Ewing did the actual work."[19] George Work said that he was at his home in Jackson, Mississippi, in May 1862, when McDaniel was building torpedoes. Francis M. Ewing, McDaniel's colleague, reported that he worked with McDaniel in torpedo research and development in April 1862.

Brown, understanding the strategic value of the Yazoo River for Vicksburg's survival, directed McDaniel to go there and begin his torpedo trials. Someone, possibly Brown or Kennon, suggested to McDaniel that he could be executed as a guerrilla if he was captured by Union forces because he wore no uniform and had no military position. McDaniel and Ewing applied for, and received on August 22, 1862, commissions as acting masters in the Confederate navy. Their appointment for secret service stated:

> Mr. F. M. Ewing and Z. McDaniel have been strongly recommended to the Department for perilous service, I have given their appointments as Acting Masters to report to you privately for secret service.
>
> They will detail their plans for using submarine batteries and you will grant them such aid as your judgment may approve in executing their plans. They propose nothing expensive, but think they can float secure longside of an enemies vessel and place and explode a torpedo to sink it. I deem it proper to afford such adventurous spirits the opportunity to test their skill and judgment, and you will please aid them accordingly by and approve their necessary bills, to be paid by your disbursement officer at Jackson.[20]

An acting master was a line officer of the grade next below that of lieutenant, the equivalent of today's navy lieutenant (junior grade).[21] Before his contact with McDaniel, Ewing fought as an independent private in Company A, Twelfth Mississippi Regiment, the Raymond Fencibles.[22] But he had lost one arm and, after having fought with a specially rigged Maynard carbine for a time, sought other duties.

In the late summer and autumn months of 1862, McDaniel's experiments with torpedoes were not bothered by Union forays into the Yazoo River because the water level in the river during that season was too low to support the draft of the gunboats. David D. Porter later described the situation: "Flag Officer Davis at first determined to occupy the Yazoo River, and from thence carry on operations against the enemy, but he found that nothing could be done in the Yazoo at low water, and besides the enemy had built formidable barricades [Weldon's raft], well defended by heavy batteries [Higgins'], at Haines' Bluff, some miles about the mouth of the river; and with these he had no sufficient force to contend."[23]

Unfortunately, this was also the fever season, when malaria and yellow fever ran rampant through the sloughs, marshes, and bayous of the Mississippi backwaters. McDaniel did not escape the sickness, and it would plague his efforts and sap his health for months to come. In late fall, however, the rains began, and the river level rose. Porter's fleet, idle at Cairo, Illinois, being refitted and repaired for upcoming action, would certainly arrive in the late fall months.

The Confederates were using several schemes to deny the potential use of the Yazoo to the Union flotilla. Approximately twenty-two miles up the river from its mouth at the Mississippi, high bluffs rise up suddenly from the river plain. The Yazoo winds through miles of flat river plain and swamp until the bluffs are encountered. The first of these bluffs upriver is Snyder's Bluff, the location of Snyder's Mill. About three miles farther upriver, northeast of Snyder's Bluff, is Haynes' Bluff. In the Yazoo, adjacent to Snyder's Bluff, Colonel Thomas Weldon, engineer and architect, built a gigantic obstruction raft, shaped like the letter "W," across the river to prevent Union vessels from passing that point and continuing upriver to Yazoo City.[24] The raft was covered by fire from artillery pieces commanded by Colonel Edward Higgins on the heights above the river. Weldon, a fifty-one-year-old bachelor born in Ireland, came to Canada with his parents and his brother George, also born in Ireland. In Canada, a third brother, William, was born. The Weldons moved to Natchez, Mississippi, in 1835 and settled there. Before the war, Weldon designed and built the Warren County Courthouse at Vicksburg.[25] His background in engineering prepared him well for the construction of the raft at Snyder's Bluff.

Approximately four miles downriver from Weldon's raft (eighteen miles upstream from the Mississippi), McDaniel and Ewing, with a crew they enlisted, were attempting to place working torpedoes in the Yazoo. Thus any ship attempting to go up the river would first have to engage McDaniel's torpedoes and then slow for Weldon's barrier. Both actions would make the boats highly vulnerable to fire from the batteries on Snyder's Bluff or from mobile, horse-drawn light artillery along the Confederate-controlled riverbank.

The attempt to build torpedoes was not immediately successful. One major problem was to find a suitable ignition system that would reliably detonate black powder, from a distance, under water. Several ignition systems were known at that time, but the knowledge apparently was not widespread. As early as 1841, Samuel Colt, inventor of the revolver, patented and successfully detonated electrically fired torpedoes in the Hudson River.[26] On Colt's first try, July 4, 1842, he sank the aged gunboat USS *Boxer* in New York Harbor. At a second trial on October 14, 1842, he sank the three-hundred-ton brig *Volta*. Confident from these successes, he invited President John Tyler, his cabinet, and some military officials to the Potomac River, near Washington, on April 13, 1843. There, using his electrically detonated torpedo from five miles away, he sank a schooner. Colt owed his knowledge to a combination of Robert Fulton's stationary torpedo and Professor Robert Hare's galvanic current instruments.[27]

Matthew Fontaine Maury also experimented with different methods of detonating torpedoes. Early in the summer of 1861, he demonstrated his torpedoes for an audience of distinguished guests on the James River. On this occasion, his torpedo consisted of "two small kegs of rifle powder, weighted to sink a few feet below the surface. They were fitted with hair triggers and friction primers, and thirty feet of lanyard attached to the triggers connected to the keys." These were drift torpedoes designed to flow with the river current until fouled against a boat's bow, anchor chain, or hull. When fouled, the line pulled the igniter wire from the friction primer, detonating the torpedo. A few months later, Maury, supported by Governor John Letcher of Virginia, opened an office at Ninth and Bank streets in Richmond and scrounged galvanic batteries, known as Wollastons, from the Richmond Medical College and later the University of Virginia. Galvanic cells were not compact devices. Maury described the Wollastons he used as follows: "For batteries we have 21

Wollastons, each trough containing 18 pairs of plates, zinc and wire, 10 × 12 inches."[28]

Gaston Planté invented the first secondary electric cell. It consisted of two lead sheets separated by rubber strips and immersed in sulfuric acid. On being charged, the surface of one lead sheet became spongy lead and the other became lead dioxide. In the Wollastons used by Maury, the plates were zinc and probably copper wire immersed in sulfuric acid. In 1816, William Wollaston created his battery using copper plates doubled around zinc plates with a space between the plates. The plates were then submerged in dilute sulfuric acid to generate the electrical current. When the batteries were not in use, the plates could be withdrawn and saved for future use.[29] With these devices in hand, Maury placed electrically fired torpedoes in the James River. He did encounter some problems:

> To obtain insulated wire, of which the South had none, an agent was sent secretly to New York, but without success, and as there was neither factory nor material for its manufacture in the Confederacy, the difficulties of preparing electric torpedoes . . . seemed insuperable, until by a remarkable piece of good fortune, in the following spring [1862], it happened that the enemy, attempting to lay [a line of insulated wire] across Chesapeake Bay were forced to abandon the attempt and left their wire to the mercy of the waves, which cast it upon the beach near Norfolk, where, by the kindness of a friend, it was secured for Captain Maury's use.[30]

Uninsulated wire would ground out the instant it touched the water or earth and fail to transmit the current so insulated wire, of the proper gauge and thus resistance for the distance traveled, was necessary to carry the electric charge to the ignition bridge inside the explosive charge. Maury, however, did not abandon his nonelectrical friction-primer-fired devices but continued to use them primarily as drift mines. Some of his further experiments showed the unique problems faced with these devices. Using a burning shot fuse inside a torpedo, he discovered that the fuses burned reliably at a depth of fifteen feet but would not burn at a depth of twenty feet. He attributed this to the water pressure at the various depths.[31]

It is unknown to what extent, if at all, the details of the ignition systems were transmitted to the western river area. Brown, however, was well acquainted with torpedoes and with Maury. Before the war, during their United States Navy service, Brown served with Maury at the United States Naval Observatory.[32] In August 1861, while at Norfolk, Virginia,

Brown wired Major General Leonidas K. Polk, then commanding Department no. 2 at Memphis: "Professor Maury, CS Navy, tells me that he is coming west to plant submarine batteries or magazines. There is no place from Cairo to New Orleans, in my opinion, so suitable for these as at the lower point of Randolph Bluffs."[33] Randolph Bluffs were part of the Mississippi River bluff line on the east side of the river about twenty miles below Cairo, Illinois, near Columbus, Kentucky. Although Maury did not make the trip west, Brown did, when he was later assigned to naval duties on the Mississippi River. Maury designed and built the torpedoes for shipment to Columbus, Kentucky, to be implanted according to his directions.

In March 1862, Union troops, alerted to the possible presence of land and naval mines, cautiously proceeded along Elliott's Mill Road and Clinton Road, two main roads into Columbus from the north. Along both roads, they found clusters of electrically detonated land mines; the galvanic batteries and telegraph key firing systems were hidden in nearby caves. Further inspection by the Union troops located the naval mines, also electrically wired with the galvanic cells and keys in caves along the river.[34]

Another Confederate torpedo inventor was Brigadier General Gabriel James Raines. Raines, a fifty-eight-year-old West Point graduate, wounded Seminole War veteran, and army lieutenant colonel when the war began, resigned his commission when his native North Carolina seceded. He always was a tinkerer and had something of a reputation for experimenting with explosives. He was catapulted into notoriety in 1862, when land mines he developed blew up some Union cavalry personnel near Williamsburg, Virginia, during operations there. In addition to the outraged cries from the North, the South's Lieutenant General James Longstreet joined in decrying the barbarity of such weapons. Raines appealed over the head of Longstreet, and Secretary of War George Randolph brought him into the War Department to direct the use of submarine batteries in the James and Appomattox rivers. After much squabbling, in May 1863, he was made head of the new secret Confederate Torpedo Bureau.[35]

Jefferson Davis wrote in his memoirs after the war with glowing praise for the devices, which obviously aided the defensive posture of the South. He noted that "the secret of all his [Gabriel Raines's] future success consisted in the sensitive primer, which is unrivaled by any other means to explode torpedoes or sub-terra shells." Describing the variety of torpedoes, he wrote: "The torpedoes were made of the most ordinary material generally, as, beer-barrels fixed with conical heads, coated within and without with rosin dissolved in coal-tar; some were made of cast-iron, copper, or tin; and glass demijohns were used. There were three essentials to success, viz., the sensitive fuse-primer, a charge of sixty pounds of gunpowder, and actual contact between the torpedo and the bottom of the vessel."[36]

Contact with the hull or side of the target vessel was a critical element not understood by some practitioners. R. O. Crowley, General Raines's electrician, reported that "experiments soon demonstrated, however, that fifty pounds of powder in from ten to fifteen feet of water would scarcely do any harm . . . we . . . decided that a tank containing two thousands pounds of cannon-powder was sure to destroy utterly a ship of any size at a depth of not more than thirty feet." Crowley went on to discuss the attack on the USS *Minnesota* on April 9, 1864, at Newport News, Virginia: "The launch [torpedo boat with a spar torpedo on the bow] perceptibly rebounded, so that at the instant of the explosion, which was not simultaneous with the blow, a cushion of water intervened between the torpedo and the hull of the *Minnesota*, thus weakening the effect and probably saving the ship."[37] The reason for this situation was that water, unlike earth or air, is not compressible. The energy released by the same explosion in all three media is the same, however. Because water cannot be compressed, and thus absorb energy, it transmits the energy of the explosion as shock waves. When an explosive under water is placed in contact with wood, such as timber or the hull of a wooden ship, the energy released by the explosion seeks the path of least resistance through the wood, which is compressible. If the explosion is large enough, the hull will cave in. The farther the explosive is from direct contact with the hull, the more a tamping (deadening) effect is created by the water, between the explosion and the hull, causing the explosive force to seek the next path of least resistance, toward the surface of the water. The explosion's effect on the hull is then weakened. Thus not only was it necessary to have direct contact with the hull of the vessel, but the charge had to be far enough below the surface of the water that it would not seek to escape via the surface of the water.

The sensitive fuse primer mentioned by Davis was also described in detail by Crowley: "Our fuses were made by taking a piece of quill, half an inch long, and filling it with fulminate of mercury. Each end of the quill was sealed with beeswax, after fixing a fine platinum wire through the center of the quill and connecting . . . the protruding ends of the platinum with insulated copper wire . . . the [fuse] opening [in the case of the metal torpedo] was then fitted with a screw plug, in which there were two holes for the passage of the wires and packed with greased cotton waste to prevent leakage of water inside."[38] The electrical current passing through the copper wire would, through resistance, heat the thin platinum wire and generate enough heat to explode the heat-sensitive fulminate of mercury. When the fulminate of mercury exploded, it would set off the main charge of black powder. This was an electrically detonated fuse and not the type used by McDaniel. McDaniel used artillery friction primers.

Friction primers were in common use in both armies and navies by the end of 1862.[39] Simply constructed, they were "a copper tube filled with powder; at the top of the tube was soldered a short tube containing a compound of antimony sulphide and potassium chlorate; lying in that composition was a roughened wire; the other end of the wire was twisted into a loop so that a lanyard could be hooked on to it."[40] They were compact, easy to use, and more moisture-resistant than the older percussion cap method of firing artillery, which operated much like the firing mechanism of the cap-lock musket. The friction primer was placed in the ignition hole on the top of the artillery piece and the lanyard attached to the friction primer's pull wire. A hard tug on the lanyard pulled the "roughened" wire through the explosive chemical composition in the primer. The friction of the wire being pulled through the chemical composition caused the composition to ignite, in turn igniting a small gunpowder charge in the remainder of the tube. The tube shape of the primer directed the ignited composition down the tube and into the main explosive charge, detonating the charge.

The 1862 Army Ordnance manual described the exact method of constructing friction primers:

> The friction-primer for cannon is a small brass tube filled with gunpowder, which is ignited by drawing a rough wire briskly through friction-composition, contained in a smaller tube inserted into the first near the top and soldered at right angles to it. A lanyard, with a hook attached, is used to ignite the primer.
>
> The friction-primer is composed of 1 large tube; 1 short tube; 1 wire rubber; friction-composition; musket powder; wax.
>
> The long tube is made from a circular disk of No. 19 sheet brass, 0.62 inch

in diameter, by means of a series of 5 punches and dies, gradually diminishing in size to the last, which is of the required size of the tube. The brass must be annealed before each punching.

The tube is cut to the prescribed length, measuring from the closed end, by means of a circular saw, and the holes for the short tube and wire rubber are drilled, and the burrs removed. Length of the long tube, 1.75 inch; exterior diameter, .19 inch; interior diameter, .175 inch; diameter of holes, .15 inch and .06 inch.

The short tube is formed from the long one by using two additional punches and dies, reducing the size each time. It is cut to the proper length by circular saws placed at the required distance apart and the burr removed by rolling in a barrel. Length of short tube, 0.44 inch; exterior diameter, 0.15 inch; interior diameter, .133 inch.

One end of the short tube is dipped into solution of chloride of zinc, inserted in the hole drilled in the long tube, heated to a redness in the flame of a spirit-lamp, and soldered with soft solder; it is then washed and dried.

The wire rubber is made of No. 16 brass wire, annealed, cut to the proper length, and pressed flat at one end by a machine for that purpose. The flat end is trimmed by a punch and die with dentated edges, and the tip is annealed in the flame of a spirit-lamp. Length of wire, 3.4 inches; length of flattened end, 0.65 inch.

The friction-composition is made of 2 parts of the sulphuret of antimony and 1 part of the chlorate of potassa, moistened with gummed water—50 grains of gum arabic in 2 ounces of water to 1 pound of composition.

The materials are first pulverized separately, mixed together dry, moistened with the gum-water, and ground in an iron mill, such as is used for grinding paint.

The small tube is charged by pressing the open end in the friction-composition spread on a flat piece of iron and brought to the consistency of soft putty, the long tube being closed its whole length with a wooden or metal plug.

A conical hole is made in the composition, while yet moist, with a conical drift, and the surplus composition removed; the wire rubber is passed through the short tube and through the small hole in the long tube, the round end first, leaving the annealed tip projecting out of the open end, which is then closed by pressing the top and bottom together firmly with pincers, and bending the tip against the bottom.

The end of the wire rubber is doubled on itself and twisted, leaving a loop 0.2 inch in diameter, and then bent alongside the long tube for packing.

The head of the long tube, including the short tube and the joint, is dipped into shellac varnish colored with lampblack.

When dry, the long tube is filled with musket-powder and closed with beeswax mixed with 1/3 its weight of pitch.

Both ends are touched with varnish and the tube thoroughly dried.[41]

The explosive used in torpedoes was black powder, also known as gunpowder. Black powder, typically, is a composition of saltpeter (potassium nitrate), or sodium nitrate, seventy-five parts by weight, sulfur, ten parts by weight; and charcoal, fifteen parts by weight. Technically, black powder does not explode, it burns. As it burns, it creates a gas. As the gas is created, pressure develops until it reaches the point that, if contained, it bursts its container. The heaving, or pushing, effect of the sudden release of gas pressure causes the damage. The burning speed of black powder, and therefore its strength, is controlled by the size of its granules. Large grains burn more slowly than small grains and are less sudden in their action, with an average burning rate of about 1,312 feet per second. Cannon powder of the type used by McDaniel in his torpedoes had granules of 0.25 inch to 0.35 inch in size.[42] Black powder is also very hygroscopic (absorbs moisture readily) and cannot burn if it is exposed to adequate moisture. It can, however, be dried out and reused because it does not deteriorate, even with age. Black powder is extremely flammable and is sensitive to spark, heat, or flame, including static spark.

2

A Torpedo Exploded and Tore the Boat Fearfully

November 1862–12 December 1862

Early in the war, the Union army exercised command over certain boats, including the ironclads, that were used for military operations in the Mississippi River area because it was thought that naval forces would operate only in support of ground forces. Commander David D. Porter wrote that "there does not seem to have been a man in the Cabinet at that time who knew the difference between a gun-boat and a transport."[1] In October 1862, after much insistence on the part of the U.S. Navy, Mississippi River boat operations, now to be known as the Mississippi Squadron, were placed under the control of Rear Admiral David Farragut. Rear Admiral Charles H. Davis was replaced by Acting Rear Admiral David D. Porter as commander of the upper Mississippi River fleet. Because the river water level was still low in October and there was no naval action, Porter decided to order all of his vessels except the *Benton* and the *Carondelet* to Cairo, Illinois, for repairs. The *Carondelet* had been just repaired after her disastrous run-in with the *Arkansas* and was left on station near Vicksburg.

Following his promotion, Porter traveled to Washington, D.C., where he met with President Lincoln. During that meeting, Lincoln told Porter that Major General John A. McClernand, a native Kentuckian who is more commonly associated with Illinois, was in Springfield, Illinois, raising an army with which he intended to take Vicksburg. Lincoln encouraged Porter to assist McClernand vigorously in the effort to reduce Vicksburg.[2] McClernand, however, was seen as not fully competent by several senior Union officers, among them Porter and Major General U.S. Grant.

When Porter returned to the Mississippi, he immediately wired Grant, now at Holly Springs, Mississippi, about the news from Lincoln concerning McClernand's plans for Vicksburg. Within a couple of days, Grant arrived in Cairo, where he met with Porter. At this meeting, which lasted only half an hour, it was decided that Grant would move to Grenada, Mississippi. They believed that this action would cause Lieutenant General John C. Pemberton to move from Vicksburg to engage Grant's forces in an attempt to hold them until Confederate reinforcements could arrive at Vicksburg. With Pemberton thus away from Vicksburg, the town could be attacked by Porter's fleet and General William T. Sherman's forces (about thirty thousand men, moving from Sherman's present position in Memphis, augmented by another force of ten thousand men from Helena, Arkansas, whom Sherman would pick up on the way to Vicksburg). The naval part of this action would require reconnaissance up the Yazoo River because Sherman's intention was to attack Vicksburg from its northern side, through Chickasaw Bayou.

Porter and Grant's fear that McClernand would arrive and dictate tactics caused them to act precipitously. Their desire for Sherman to make a frontal assault on Walnut Hills, a bluff line running from Vicksburg northeast to Snyder's Bluff, which would probably result in the loss of many men and large amounts of material, stemmed more from their fear of McClernand's possible success, giving him more command influence in the theater of operations, than from a sane evaluation of the available intelligence regarding strength, disposition, and intentions of the enemy. Grant would later write in his *Memoirs*: "My action in sending Sherman back was expedited by a desire to get him in command of the forces separated from my direct supervision. I feared that delay might bring McClernand, who was his senior and who had authority from the President and Secretary of War to exercise that particular command—and independently."[3] As it turned out, lack of communications between Grant and Sherman caused their plan to fail, and the necessary Confederate forces were not pulled out of Vicksburg.

On November 19, 1862, Porter alerted Walke to prepare his flotilla to descend to the Yazoo River. On November 21, he ordered Walke to proceed with his entire force, less the *Benton* and the *General Bragg*, the Confederate ram captured at Memphis and now a Union vessel, to the Vicksburg area. He further ordered Walke to conduct the necessary reconnaissance up the Yazoo to determine the condition (i.e., depth) of the river and of Confederate forces in the area. Any Confederate obstacles, such as batteries, were to be reduced by the gunboats preparatory to Sherman's landing. If the water level was too low, Walke was to use the tinclads *Marmora* and *Signal*, which drew only about three and a half feet of water, for the reconnaissance. Tinclads, unlike ironclads, had very light armor, sometimes only about an inch thick, designed to protect against rifle fire but useless against any large weapon such as a naval gun or an artillery piece. At times, their armor was augmented by cotton bales, logs, or other items to help increase the stopping power of the armor. With these lightly armored, shallow-draft vessels, Walke was to keep the Confederate presence in the lower Yazoo at a minimum until Sherman could arrive and land his troops for the assault on Vicksburg. On November 22, Porter ordered the *Cairo* to report to Walke at Helena, Arkansas. On November 24, he ordered the *Queen of the West* and the *Switzerland*, both Ellet rams, to report to Walke as well. On November 25, Walke's advance party, consisting of the *Signal*, *Marmora*, *Carondelet*, and *Mound City*, left Helena for the Yazoo and arrived at Milliken's Bend, Louisiana, approximately twenty miles up the Mississippi River from Vicksburg, on November 28. The following day, Walke ordered the *Signal* and the *Marmora* to conduct a reconnaissance of the Yazoo with particular attention to hydrographic soundings and Confederate positions. The ships advanced cautiously, finding only one spot in the lower Yazoo where the ironclads could not cross because of the water level. They made their way to the vicinity of Snyder's Bluff and Drumgould's Bluff (the bluff extending south from Snyder's Bluff toward Vicksburg), about three or four miles above McDaniel's torpedo camp, and observed the construction of Confederate entrenchments at those locations. After making these observations, they returned to report to Walke.[4]

After they returned to the mouth of the Yazoo, the water level in the river began falling and Walke ordered the flotilla back to the deep water at Milliken's Bend. After six days, the water level rose again, and Walke moved the flotilla back to the mouth of the Yazoo on December 5. The *Marmora* and the *Signal* conducted further reconnaissances of the Yazoo.

Farther north, on December 5, the *Cairo*, after a series of delays brought about by bureaucratic squabbling among various commanders as to the proper use of the boat, ran into a severe snowstorm and was forced to dock at Helena, Arkansas, for two days. On December 6, when the snow slackened, the *Cairo* resumed her southern course. That same day, the *Queen of the West* arrived at the mouth of the Yazoo ready for action. Finally, on December 8, at 2:00 P.M., the *Cairo* arrived at the mouth of the Yazoo to complete the complement of vessels. The stage was set for conflict in the Yazoo.[5]

The early December weather was typical. Twelve hours' work could be done if a man toiled from first light until last light in the cold.[6] The cold nights alternated with only slightly warmer days. Sometimes it rained or snowed and nothing could be done except to sit and wait out the storm. Sometimes there was fog on the river and in the swamps. The river water was cold enough to numb hands and feet. Working in the small, shallow boats was difficult enough, let alone while handling a torpedo fused and filled with cannon powder. With the rise in the river, everyone knew it was only a matter of time before the Union fleet tried to ascend the Yazoo again.

Problems abounded in McDaniel's torpedo crew. In addition to the deteriorating weather, the torpedoes were not reliable. McDaniel's plan for detonating the torpedoes involved using a container filled with cannon powder. David Curry, in his statement to Weldon in 1864, wrote that the container "was arranged with a tube extending from the chamber in which the powder was contained. This tube was encased in a wooden box within which was a lock similar to that of a gun. The trigger could be worked by wires. Ignition was to be effected by a percussion cap. The case around the tube could not be made watertight. Therefore the powder became wet in a short time after being submerged."[7] Wires ran from the gunlock to torpedo pits on shore, where they were manually fired by concealed crew members. Time and again over the months, the torpedoes did not fire. Admiral Porter reported the failure of Confederate torpedoes in a letter to Gideon Welles as a backhanded excuse for why Lieutenant Commander Thomas O. Selfridge, Jr., lost the USS *Cairo* to one. He commented that "these torpedoes have proved so harmless heretofore (not one exploding out of the many hundreds that have been planted by the rebels) that officers have not felt that respect for them to which they are entitled."[8]

McDaniel was working in cooperation with Commander Isaac Brown.

McDaniel's relationship with Governor Pettus, the joint Confederate and Mississippi state lines of command, and McDaniel's own independent attitude, however, left him with no immediate supervisor. Brown detailed some of his sailors, who no longer had boats, to assist McDaniel in torpedo work on the Yazoo.[9] Of McDaniel's entire crew of about fifteen men the following can be identified: Francis M. Ewing, D. M. Currie, David Curry,[10] George B. Stewart,[11] Isaac S. Johnston, Charles T. Brooke,[12] T. O. Davis,[13] John Beggs,[14] Francis Marion Tucker, James J. Dees,[15] [Samuel] Sprawls,[16] John C. Stancil.[17]

Brown became concerned because there were no operable torpedoes in the Yazoo and Union gunboats (*Marmora* and *Signal* on November 29 and December 5) had ascended the Yazoo as far as Snyder's Bluff without being seriously hindered or stopped by Confederate defenses. Francis Tucker, in his statement to Weldon in 1864, reported that Major General Martin Luther Smith had expressed his dissatisfaction that the torpedoes were not operable in early December.[18] During the first week of December 1862, Brown sent Acting Gunner I. Burton to McDaniel's camp.[19] According to the statement of Edward C. Blake, Burton stopped at Weldon's camp on his journey from Yazoo City to McDaniel's camp. Burton's mission, according to Blake, was "to ascertain why the enemy could pass the torpedoes which Mr. McDaniel had been placing in the river without being injured by them and if possible to make them effective."[20] Burton left Weldon's camp and continued his trek to McDaniel's camp.

Burton, McDaniel, and the crew struggled with the problem of the wet powder and unreliable ignition systems but to no avail. Burton was away from McDaniel's camp for two days. Blake, who was still with Weldon at Snyder's Bluff, wrote, "After the elaps of several days, Burton returned to the bluff and stated that there was no hope of success in consequence of the deficiency of the torpedoes and that further attempts to injure the enemy should be a waste of time."[21]

According to Blake and Weldon in later correspondence, Weldon thought of a way to make the torpedoes operable. Weldon took Burton into Vicksburg, where they procured "materials" and returned to Weldon's camp. The next day, Weldon obtained artillery friction primers from Colonel Edward Higgins, whose guns covered Weldon's barrier raft from the heights of Haynes' Bluff. Blake, a carpenter, then made some "appliances" to assist Burton with the new torpedoes. These were probably fuses because to make a complete torpedo and then transport it four miles over rough terrain was too risky.

Burton returned to McDaniel's camp with Blake on about December 9 or 10, with the materials to make torpedoes, the most important of which were the artillery friction primers. Using the friction primers instead of the percussion cap locks as they had before, Burton, McDaniel, and the torpedo crew built new torpedoes. David Curry, one of the torpedo crew who wrote to Weldon in 1864, reported on the exact construction of the torpedo:

> The powder was put into the demijohn. The primer was inserted in a wooden shaft. This shaft extended in the powder to below the center. Its top end came a small distance up the neck of the demijohn. A groove was cut in the side of the shaft for the wires which was attached to the primers and forced through the gum extending some distance outside of the demijohn. To this wire could be attached a line or wire. The gum was fitted tight into the neck of the demijohn, one piece resting on the top of the shaft. On this was poured melted wax. The neck was then nearly filled with tallow. On top of this was fitted another piece of gum which was well secured by means of wires bound round the neck of the demijohn and lashed over the top of the gum.[22]

Alfred Thayer Mahan, writing long after the war and apparently relying on postwar correspondence with Isaac Brown, said, "The torpedoes by which the Cairo was sunk were merely demijohns filled with powder and ignited by a common friction primer rigidly secured inside. To the primer was fastened a wire passing through a water-tight cork of gutta percha and plaster of paris."[23] It is possible that in the cold water of the Yazoo River in December the tallow and wax took on the consistency of plaster of paris. "White lead," in powder form, is basic lead carbonate ($2PbCO_3$ Pb[OH]). When combined with oil in proper amounts, it forms a pliable, waterproof putty. Although Curry mentions having white lead, no one mentions its use on the torpedoes. Gutta percha is the sap of the Sapodilla family of plants, usually the *Palaguium gutta*, a native of Malaysia. The sap is processed to make a tough, rubberlike gum. The gum is pliable when placed in hot water. When it cools, it retains the shape in which it is formed. In the middle of the nineteenth century, gutta percha was used for insulating electric wires. Tallow is the solid, rendered fat of animals, usually sheep or cattle. It is very greasy and water-resistant. The wax used was probably beeswax, a common item in 1862.

Walke's small force finally was completely on station at the mouth of the

Yazoo River by December 8. In addition to the *Carondelet*, it consisted of the ironclads *Cairo*, commanded by Lieutenant Commander Thomas O. Selfridge, Jr., *Baron de Kalb*,[24] commanded by Lieutenant Commander Jonathan G. Walker, and *Pittsburg*, commanded by Acting Volunteer Lieutenant William G. Hoel; the Ellet ram *Queen of the West*, commanded by army Captain Edward W. Sutherland;[25] and two tinclads, *Marmora*, commanded by Acting Volunteer Lieutenant Robert Getty, and *Signal*, commanded by Acting Volunteer Lieutenant John Scott.

On December 11, 1862, Walke decided to have his lightly armored tinclads conduct another reconnaissance of the Yazoo River. The *Marmora* and *Signal* were chosen because of their shallow draft and given their orders. Getty and Scott cautiously made their way up the Yazoo River. After they proceeded, by their estimate, about twenty miles, they discovered some small boats along the bank of the river and several "stationary floats of various kinds" in the water. They decided that these signs indicated Confederate torpedo activity. While they were examining the devices, a torpedo exploded near the *Signal*.[26] Unknown to Getty and Scott, the torpedo was a command-detonated device (one fired intentionally by a human as opposed to a self-detonating device, which fires when disturbed by an object or an unwitting human) fired from the shore by two torpedo corps members, Francis Marion Tucker and a Mr. Sprawls. The torpedo was placed in the river by Tucker and John Beggs and rigged to be fired by pulling on a lanyard.[27]

There were reasons for the Confederate torpedo crew to be concerned because they had not tested an artillery friction primer as the firing device instead of a percussion cap lock, although the friction primer had been used in eastern waters for some time. This may have been its first use in the West. Tucker later reported that both torpedoes were detonated by pulling on a lanyard attached to friction primers embedded in the torpedoes. He noted that both exploded and that the resultant explosions had no effect on either boat. Edward Blake, the carpenter working for Weldon near Snyder's Bluff in December 1862, reported the incident involving the *Signal* as follows: "The first approach of the enemy two of the torpedoes were exploded by means of a laniard from the shore—which produced no effect other than causing the gunboats to withdraw." Some years after the war, Alfred Thayer Mahan, who himself was never on the western waters and who wrote secondhand from others' accounts, wrote about the December 11 incident: "The very first primitive idea was to explode them [the torpedoes] by pulling [the friction primer lanyard] from shore, and it is possible that the first to go off near the light-draughts [*Marmora* and *Signal*] was thus fired."[28]

The torpedo exploded near the *Signal* did no damage to the vessel, but Scott and Getty thought it best to be cautious. Both boats fired some harassing fire into the surrounding swamps and withdrew down the Yazoo to the Walke flotilla. As they left, riflemen aboard the *Marmora* fired at the floats, hoping to detonate other torpedoes. While they fired, a second torpedo exploded. Walke would later report that the musket fire detonated the torpedo, not realizing that the devices were command-detonated and that musket fire would not detonate them. Once back at the mouth of the Yazoo River, they reported the day's incident to Walke and advised him that they could remove the torpedoes, using men in open cutters, if they had sufficient naval gunfire support to suppress guerrilla small arms fire during the operation.[29] They also told him that the river had risen enough so the ironclad gunboats would have no problem navigating the Yazoo.

Acting on the report of Scott and Getty, Walke ordered most of his flotilla to prepare for an expedition in force up the Yazoo to remove the mines. Selfridge, commanding the *Cairo*, requested that he be sent on the mission. After consulting with the rest of his boat commanders, Walke decided the expedition would consist of the *Cairo*, *Pittsburg*, *Queen of the West*, *Signal*, and *Marmora*. In addition, a group of infantry sharpshooters, under the command of Acting Ensign Walter E. H. Fentress, would be on board the *Marmora*. Selfridge, as senior officer, would command the flotilla.

After the sinking of the *Cairo*, Walke stated that the order of approach was to be with the two tinclads in the lead to remove torpedoes, followed by the ram, and the rear brought up by the two ironclads. Thus the work on the torpedoes could be performed under the protective guns of the ram and the two ironclads. Walke insisted that he also told the boat commanders that "if there was any apparent danger in the execution of [his orders] to relinquish the project and return until better means could be obtained to scour the shores and drag out the torpedoes."[30] With these admonitions, the boat commanders prepared their vessels for the expedition up the Yazoo.

Even though no damage was done in the attack on the *Marmora* and the *Signal*, it had been proved that the torpedoes worked. McDaniel's crew had every reason to believe that Union boats would soon return in force. It might be too dangerous to man the torpedo pits under fire from naval artillery at a range of less than one hundred yards. The torpedo crew then renewed its work. This time, about eighteen to twenty torpedoes were set in pairs and rigged to detonate when a boat struck a trigger wire, which in turn pulled out the friction primer wire, igniting the powder charge.[31]

The torpedo arrangement can be reconstructed from contemporary accounts and from McDaniel's later patent with the Confederate Patent Office. The torpedoes were constructed much as shown in Fentress's drawing, although that drawing is wrong in several respects. The torpedoes were made as previously described by Curry and the others. A piece of wood large enough to float the torpedoes was used. This piece of wood was chosen by trial and error; the ideal size gave the arrangement a neutral buoyancy. The floats were connected to the torpedo by the fuse wires and by some string or wire arrangement wrapped around the float and the torpedo. Fentress's drawing shows an arrangement that required a positive, or at least neutral, buoyancy torpedo. If not, the torpedo in the drawing would sink to the bottom of the river because only the primer wires held it to the float. In all probability, some type of harness was arranged that held the torpedo to the float but did not interfere with the pulling action of the trigger wires.

The torpedo float was connected to a pulley, which, in turn, was attached to the weights brought by Burton. A rope attached to the float with a staple or some other device was fed through the pulley and returned to shore so the torpedo could be positioned under water. The gunboats and rams had a very shallow draft, about six feet. If the torpedoes were too far under water, the ships would pass over them without detonating them. If the torpedoes were too high, they would be seen and destroyed. If exploded by a boat, they would expend most of their explosive force out through the surface of the water and do minimal damage to the boat. The pulleys allowed the torpedoes to be placed in the river without regard to the condition of the river bottom or the topography. If a simple rope and weight method were used, the torpedo crew could not accurately determine where the torpedoes would float at rest. With the pulleys, however, once the torpedoes were in the river, the ropes were played in or out through the pulleys to raise or lower the torpedoes to the required depth. The depth adjustment was checked with a pole or line of the required length. One problem was that no one wanted to get into the cold river with the torpedoes.

According to Ewing, the torpedoes were set about a boat width, or fifty feet, apart. The obvious expectation was that a boat would engage the trigger line, pulling the torpedoes against the hull on each side of the boat, and detonate the torpedoes when they came into contact with the hull.

McDaniel and Ewing hoped that with the new supplies from Weldon they could make the Yazoo torpedo defenses extremely hazardous for the Union fleet. Weldon, however, had not supplied any cannon powder for the torpedoes.[32] McDaniel went to Vicksburg on December 11 and once again wired Governor Pettus: "Please come to Yazoo River tomorrow. Forward all the powder you can spare. Don't fail to come. Tis highly necessary."[33] McDaniel had high hopes for the new torpedoes, but he desperately needed the cannon powder that Pettus could bring. McDaniel waited in Vicksburg on December 12 intent on collecting equipment and material until late in the day. Ewing remained at the torpedo camp as officer in charge.[34]

On the evening of December 11, 1862, while anchored in the Mississippi River near the mouth of the Yazoo, Captain Henry Walke held a meeting aboard his ship, the *Carondelet*. It was attended by the commanders of four of the five boats that would ascend the Yazoo the next day to find and destroy the torpedoes that had been reported by Getty and Scott. Getty, Scott, *Pittsburg* commander Lieutenant William G. Hoel, and *Cairo* commander Lieutenant Commander Thomas O. Selfridge all listened to Walke's verbal orders concurring their mission. Following the meeting, they returned to their vessels to prepare them to move the next morning. Captain Edward Sutherland of the *Queen of the West* wrote to his commanding officer, Colonel Ellet, on December 12: "I yesterday waited upon Captain Walke (the officer in command here) and asked permission to go on any enterprises that might be in contemplation by him. My request was favorably received and granted. I was then informed that a recent expedition up the Yazoo River had developed some torpedoes or infernal machines placed in the channel to destroy our boats, and that he intends to make an effort to remove them today."[35]

Walke later reported that he "cautioned the commanding officers of all the boats of the expedition (being present), and Captain Selfridge in particular, to be very careful not to run their vessels in among the torpedoes, but to avoid the channel where they were set; to scour the shore with small boats and haul the torpedoes on shore, and destroy them before proceeding farther up the river. . . . These instructions I repeated positively; and also, that if there was any apparent danger in the execution of them to relinquish the project and return until better means could be obtained to scour the shores and drag out the torpedoes." Walke obviously had no idea how the torpedoes were fused because dragging one with the detonating system intact might detonate it. The condition and the sensitivity of the friction primer were additional factors that no one could estimate. In a letter to Porter after the sinking of the *Cairo* he referred to it as "that sad occasion which would have been avoided if my instructions had been followed."[36]

Other commanders on the scene also remembered Walke's orders. Hoel later recalled, "You [Walke] also cautioned particularly about running any unnecessary risk either in the loss of life or boats, and should there occur any probability of either, the expedition was to return, *as you did not consider it of any vital importance whether the obstructions were removed*" (emphasis added). If removing the torpedoes was not important, why take the risk? Any military expedition during war risks loss of life and material to enemy action. Walke had been ordered to remove the mines before Sherman's intended assault so it is doubtful that he told his commanders that it did not matter if the mines were removed. Porter certainly remembered his written orders to Walke: "Send on the *Signal* and *Marmora* with some good marksmen besides their crews; let them hold on to all they can until you can get your large vessels in. *We must make a landing for the army at all hazard* and prevent the rebels from raising batteries, etc." (emphasis added).[37] His concern was that on December 20, 1862, Sherman's infantry forces would embark on transport steamers from Memphis for the land assault on Vicksburg.

Getty attempted to repeat Walke's orders verbatim: "On the evening of the 11th instant . . . we received verbal orders from you to the following import, viz: That we should start the following morning on an expedition up the Yazoo River to destroy the torpedoes placed therein . . . that we should proceed with great caution. . . . That when the point should be reached where the torpedoes were placed, the ironclads should shell the shores and the remaining vessels send their small boats along the shores and discover and destroy the lines and wires which held the torpedoes.

But, while so doing to exercise the greatest care and prudence and run no risk to life or vessels."[38]

Edward W. Sutherland, a Union army officer among naval officers of equal rank and in command of Ellet's ram *Queen of the West*, was attached to Walke's small flotilla by Porter. He requested to join the Yazoo expedition and may not originally have been expected to be present. In retrospect, he gave his version of Walke's orders: "My distinct understanding of your instruction was that the *Marmora* and the *Signal*, being light draft boats, should cautiously advance along the shore, carefully avoiding the channel, and destroy the torpedoes, while the other boats, keeping at a safe distance, should protect them with their batteries." In his report to Walke, Selfridge did not mention Walke's precautionary statements.[39] Fate had now set the stage for the arrival of the *Cairo*.

At about 8:00 A.M., December 12, 1862, the five-boat flotilla began its move from the Mississippi anchorage toward and up the Yazoo River. The order of procession had been verbally dictated by Walke the day before: *Marmora* and *Signal* to lead, followed by *Queen of the West*, *Cairo*, and *Pittsburg*. After about three and a half hours' travel, Getty in the *Marmora* overtook a small skiff in the river manned by a white man and a black man. Under interrogation, the white man admitted that his name was Jonathan Williams and he was an overseer on the Blake plantation. The black man said his name was Jonathan Blake, a servant of the plantation owner, Mrs. Blake. Jonathan Blake told the Union interrogator that Williams knew of the existence and location of the torpedoes placed near Blake's plantation. "On being closely questioned," Williams admitted that he knew where the torpedoes were located. Both men were considered prisoners and placed in irons to be delivered later to Fleet Captain A. M. Pennock at Cairo, Illinois.[40] It is not clear whether Williams and Blake were on an intelligence mission or simply unlucky. They were only a couple of miles below the torpedoes and might have been lookouts for McDaniel's crew.

The Confederates in McDaniel's crew had short warning of the approach of the Union flotilla. Ewing recalled in his claim that "on the 12th day of December last between ten and eleven o'clock of that day five of the enemys armed vessels appeared below the batteries shelling the river banks furiously. . . . When the gunboats first approached we had only fourteen men in camp near the torpedo batteries and they were unarmed. There was but one rifle in the party. Most of the encampment immediately retired beyond range of the gun boats. Some four or five only remaining in the vicinity of [Ewing] and under protection of the levee." T. O. Davis, another crew member, wrote later that "our tents were about two or three hundred yards of the [torpedo location]; we had orders to take them down and take care of ourselves as best we could, as we calculated being shelled; as they shelled us before, some of the company went to the hills about a mile off." Edward C. Blake reported that "at the approach of the enemy we retired to a camp which was out of the range of the guns." Davis and Ewing were the only two Confederate witnesses who reported on what happened next. Davis said, "I wished to see what they [the torpedoes] did and went up to the river, about a half mile, when the levy was high so I could hide myself, and have protection from the shells." "Ewing was standing on the River bank at a distance of forty to sixty yards in full view of the *Cairo* . . . and witnessed the whole scene."[41]

The *Marmora*, in the lead, was on the left (north) side of the river going up. Approximately fifty yards to the rear starboard quarter, the *Cairo* steamed up the right (south) side. Approximately two hundred yards to the rear of the *Cairo*, the *Pittsburg* ran in line with the *Cairo*. Abreast of the *Pittsburg* and on her port side, the *Queen of the West* ran behind the *Marmora*. The *Signal* was forward of the *Queen of the West* and to the rear of the *Marmora* on the same side of the river.[42]

Upon reaching the area where the torpedoes had been found the day before, the *Marmora* slowed and stopped after a torpedo float was sighted. Getty then put Fentress out in a cutter from the *Marmora* with orders to search the shores and attempt to locate the torpedo lines that ran up onto the bank. While Fentress was in the cutter, marksmen aboard the *Marmora* began firing their rifles at floating objects in the river in an attempt to detonate or break up any mines. Fentress meanwhile found a line near the shore where it came to the surface, cut it, and raised a torpedo.

When Selfridge heard the rifle fire he thought that the *Marmora* was under fire from hostile riflemen on the river. He moved the *Cairo* forward to determine the problem. The *Marmora* was partially hidden from his view by the river bend. Upon gaining full view, he called to the *Marmora* to have the riflemen cease fire. His request went unheeded and there was no response from the *Marmora*. Selfridge then put out one of the *Cairo*'s own cutters with some of his crew aboard. This cutter, too, began searching for torpedo lines.

Fentress recovered the torpedo that he brought up, took it on his cutter, and foolishly returned with it to the *Marmora*, where he took it on board and began destroying it.[43] The cutter crew from the *Cairo* found only an old torpedo hull from the previous day. Selfridge then ordered the *Marmora* to proceed forward. The *Cairo*, in the meantime, drifted in toward shore, bow first. Selfridge backed up the *Cairo*, straightened the ship upstream, and proceeded forward. The *Cairo* moved only about half the length of the *Marmora* when she struck a torpedo trigger line.

Selfridge noted that one torpedo exploded "close to my port quarter" and a second "apparently under my port bow—the latter so severe as to raise the guns under it some distance from the deck." Fentress, aboard the *Marmora* destroying the torpedo on deck, heard the explosion and "on looking up I saw her anchor thrown up several feet in the air." Ewing was watching from the bank and later reported: "The *Cairo* struck the trigger of the batteries at an acute angle exploding one torpedo on her left side near her bow and another on her right side amidships . . . the anchor and chain which hung on the left on the bow of the boat was thrown high above the vessel." Davis, who was hiding in the safety of the levee about one-half mile northeast of the location reported, "I heard the torpedo explode; I could not see the boat at the time; it was behind the point; there was others in sight firing continually when the torpedo exploded."[44]

Immediately after the explosion, the *Cairo* began shipping water. Within three minutes, the water was over her forecastle the length of the ship. In an attempt to save his boat, Selfridge ran it into the shore. He ordered crewmen to get out a hawser and run the hawser around a nearby willow tree. As the ship continued to take on water, he began removing his sick and wounded, as well as some small arms.[45] A cutter from the *Pittsburg* arrived with a special tarpaulin to seal the hole but was too late. Given no other option, Selfridge gave the last command, "Abandon ship." The *Queen of the West* came alongside and took off most of the *Cairo*'s crew. Others were taken off by the various small boats from the other gunboats. Selfridge was taken aboard the *Pittsburg*, where he resumed command of the flotilla. No one aboard the *Cairo* was killed in this action, but several received wounds. Within twelve minutes, by most accounts, the *Cairo* slid under the chocolate-colored waters of the Yazoo into thirty-six feet of water to rest for one hundred years. Sutherland tore down the *Cairo*'s smokestacks and her light spars in an effort to hide her location from the Confederates on shore for fear they would raise her guns and use them against the Union fleet.

Ewing reported that "she struggled a moment in the whirlpool created by the explosion—a cloud of white smoke arose above her, when she is instantly sunk. Only three of her crew were observed to float on the surface. . . . The steamer below the Cairo [the *Pittsburg*] threw out small boats—landing men on both sides of the river, when [Ewing]—retired to a distance of about four hundred yards. The enemy continued to shell with all their batteries, while their men in small boats apparently surveyed the water and river banks in the vicinity of the wreck and searched for and destroyed some of our remaining torpedoes."[46]

In addition to his official report to Walke, Sutherland wrote another report, which he referred to as "semi-official," to his boat's commander, Colonel Charles Ellet:

> This morning at an early hour the fleet got under way in the order above indicated, Captain Selfridge of the Cairo being in command. While moving up the river I let the boat immediately in advance lead me a few hundred yards, in conformity with the instructions of Captain Walke. But Captain Selfridge soon came alongside and ordered me to proceed faster. I replied that I should govern the speed of this boat by that of the boat preceding.
>
> Nevertheless, he repeated the order so often and crowded me so close that I found it difficult to avoid running into the boats in advance. I have never seen an expedition conducted with so little order. Had it been necessary for the boats in advance to stop or back, they could not have done so, from the inevitable certainty of being run into by this boat. I could not but feel for them; merciless torpedoes in front, and an equally inexorable ram in their rear. However, we arrived in sight of the enemy's fort [Higgins's Confederate artillery emplacements on Snyder's Bluff] without any accident. The boat in advance announced the presence of danger by firing a volley of musketry.
>
> The fleet came to a halt and commenced an irregular fire. Captain Selfridge came alongside with the Cairo and inquired of the Marmora why they did not go ahead. The answer was that they were right at the torpedoes, which was true, as we could see the buoys just before us.
>
> I now hugged the shore as close as possible and crowded the advance boats. They moved forward a little distance when peremptorily ordered by Captain Selfridge. He also advanced with the Cairo in the middle of the stream, and when about a boats length ahead of me a torpedo exploded immediately under the Cairo, blowing her almost out of water. She headed directly for the other shore, Captain Selfridge crying that he was sinking and calling for me to come to his assistance. It is proper to remark that the boats now, all of them, were immediately together, one or two of them almost directly between this boat and the Cairo. I now received as many orders, perhaps, as there were officers on the other boats, all conflicting, of course. My officers were, as might be expected, much confused, and perhaps

hesitated to pass over unseen dangers against which they could make no defence. We were in sight of the rebel fort, perhaps an enemy all around us, and in a narrow river filled with torpedoes. I do not complain, then, that my first orders were not obeyed; therefore, after reestablishing order and discipline, I, for the third time, commanded the pilot to go alongside the sinking boat, torpedoes or no torpedoes; and then asked him if he distinctly understood the command. He answered in the affirmative, and the order was promptly obeyed. I have risked the safety of this boat today, from motives of humanity, and acted according to my best judgment.

I received orders from all the other boats, nearly, some which were "go up", and some to "keep away", none of which I gave any attention to. In crossing over to the Cairo, I used all the precautions I could. I directed the gunners to train the guns over the bank, and throw shell and canister. I made fast to the Cairo, and took off over one hundred of the crew, with most of their effects, (the others left in boats). The Cairo went down in about ten minutes after the explosion, sinking nearly over the chimneys. I remained by and picked up the floating wreck and such articles as we could and then pulled down her chimneys and flagstaff.

The Cairo had just been repaired, had a full crew, and was said to be the best boat in the fleet. All true officers and soldiers engaged in this expedition must feel shame and indignation that the rebels should exult in the success of so shallow a trick. Those torpedoes could have been removed and the enterprise could and should have been eminently successful. Captain Selfridge annoyed me with some offensive orders to-day, but it was some satisfaction to hear him cry so lustily for the Ram to assist him; it was a sweet revenge for me; I do not pretend to say why the other boats did not go to his aid. . . . I regret to say that every instinct of honor forbids my following the lead of officers who, rashly, and without cause, endanger the safety of my boat, and then make me responsible if it is lost, and who have not the skill and coolness to extricate themselves from danger after heedlessly going into it.[47]

With Selfridge and his men safely aboard the other boats, landing parties were sent out in an attempt to locate and destroy the torpedo camp. Meanwhile, the boats continued to pour harassing and interdictory fire into the nearby countryside. The *Pittsburg* put out two small boats, and the crews went ashore. The *Pittsburg*'s boats were under the charge of the *Pittsburg*'s executive officer, A. J. Wilson. Wilson's crews "succeeded in dragging 12 of them [torpedoes] from the river and destroying them; he also, while on shore, found the magazine of powder and other material of which the torpedoes were manufactured, all of which he destroyed, as well as some 20 skiffs and small boats which were at the landing."[48] The Union cannoneers poured round after round of shot and shell into the surrounding area to drive off any Confederate infantry and allow Wilson's crew to do their work. Wilson's crew returned, and Selfridge ordered the small flotilla back down the river. It was now midafternoon, and he did not want to be on the river at night where they would be subject to ambush by Confederates.[49]

All Confederate reports by those involved in building the torpedoes leave no doubt that the torpedoes put into the Yazoo in mid-December 1862 by McDaniel's crew were fired by friction primers, not by galvanic cells. No Confederate source reported McDaniel even having, much less using, galvanic cells. No contemporary Union reporter who was on the Yazoo that day mentioned seeing or finding any evidence of galvanic cells or electrical detonating apparatus. If Fentress discovered banks of Wollastons on the river, he would have readily reported them. Electrical batteries were a rarity in 1862. The whole idea that McDaniel's torpedoes were fired electrically seems to come from the December 17, 1862, letter of Porter to Gideon Welles: "The torpedo which blew up the *Cairo* was evidently fired by a galvanic battery, as in some of them which were afterwards taken up. The officers followed the wires over 400 yards from the river banks and would have followed them up but for fear of surprises."[50] Porter clearly was not certain that galvanic cells were used. He also indicates that the "wires" were not completely followed to their origin. Two days later, the *Cairo*'s executive officer, Master Hiram K. Hazlett, was interviewed by a reporter from the *St. Louis Daily Democrat*. After the interview, the reporter told America that "Master H. K. Haslett thinks the torpedo was exploded by a galvanic battery."[51]

If the distance given by Porter is accurate, eight hundred yards, or almost half a mile, of insulated copper wire would have been required to make a run that far for just one torpedo. Coupled with the fact that there was virtually no insulated wire in the Confederacy and the report that there were eighteen to twenty torpedoes in the river, the galvanic cell theory is impossible.[52]

Crowley, who regularly worked with galvanic torpedoes in the East, said, "To give some idea of the many difficulties we encountered [while experimenting with electrically fired torpedoes in the summer of 1862 in Virginia], I will mention first, the scarcity of cannon powder; secondly, we had only about four miles of insulated copper wire in the entire Confederacy; thirdly, we could obtain only about four or five feet of fine-gage platinum wire. Battery material was very scarce, and acids could be purchased only from the small quantity remaining in the hands of druggists when the war broke out."[53]

Isaac Brown, writing to Stephen R. Mallory, Confederate secretary of the navy, two weeks after the sinking, said:

> The torpedo used by . . . McDaniel and Ewing . . . in the destruction of the enemys gunboat on the Yazoo River, on the 14th [sic] December 1862, was a five gallon demijohn (of glass) filled with powder—This demijohn first had a stopper of wax then a plug of India rubber through both of which ran a copper wire 1/16 of an inch in diameter. The wire was made fast to a "friction primer" properly secured inside the demijohn. This wire connected to another torpedo at some distance extending in a direction of crossing the channel. To secure these torpedoes in proper position, a rock or other suitable weight was dropped, having a pulley, or block, with sheare attached, with a line ran—One end of this line was taken a shore, the other made fast to a piece of timber sufficient to float the torpedo which in turn was made fast to the timber. By hauling on the shore end of the line the torpedo could be taken to any desired depth.[54]

It is likely that the 1/16-inch copper wire (about American Wire Gauge #14) used to connect the friction primer wire to the outside of the torpedo was assumed to be for electrical purposes.

In his after-action report, Fentress said: "As I approached it [one of the torpedoes] . . . I pushed forward to reach a line that I saw on the bank. As soon as I could I severed the line with my sword, and a large object immediately arose in the middle of the river. Pulling to it by the line, I soon discovered it to be some 'infernal machine', and upon closer examination I found a wire running from it to the shore, and was ordered . . . to cut it, which I did, and towed the torpedo to [my ship]."[55] Fentress's statement makes it plain that he cut the depth adjustment line, described by Brown and drawn by Fentress (item "A"), which ran from the torpedoes to the bank. Fentress, the officer who picked up McDaniel's torpedo, later made a drawing of his observations, which is the only known graphic representation of the torpedoes in use by McDaniel's crew.[56]

Fentress's description contains no mention of galvanic cells. In his drawing, items "D" and "E" ("wires running into the vessel containing bursting charge") are lumped together but drawn differently. Item "D" is drawn in the same manner as item "A" ("the rope by which the engine was sunk").[57] Fentress's drawing is also very consistent with Brown's description. If the torpedoes were laid in a line, as Ewing stated, then they would be connected by a line, probably a rope. To raise or lower the torpedoes in the river would require a system such as that described by Brown and drawn by Fentress. The two wires extending from the demijohn to the float in Fentress's drawing are possibly a primary and backup ignition system. If one wire did not pull out the friction primer wire, broke the primer wire, or the initial friction primer failed to function, the backup was available for an immediate second try.[58]

Brown, in an article published many years after the war, said, "I set these two enterprising men [McDaniel and Ewing] to work with a coil of small iron wire which they stretched from bank to bank."[59] This may have been the wire Fentress referred to and may have caused the assumption of electricity although cursory inspection would have shown that the wire was not insulated.

Ewing reported: "The torpedoes were anchored in the River at a distance about the width of a boat a part, they were sunk to a depth of five and half feet below the surface of the River and so arranged and located that the enemys boats, in passing up the River at that point, must necessarily run upon some one or more of the trigger drawing the friction primers and firing a torpedo and each side of the boat thereby producing instantaneous explosion and destruction of the vessel." Milton F. Perry, an expert on Confederate torpedoes, opined that "the ship struck the wire, pulling the bottles onto her sides igniting both friction primer fuses. Since the explosions occurred under the bow and on the port quarter, it appears that the *Cairo* almost missed the torpedoes, and struck the wire very near the torpedo at the right side of the channel. The bottle was held against the bow by the ship's forward motion; this in turn pulled in the second mine, which struck the port side and exploded."[60]

It is possible that the second torpedo was exploded by the pulling effect of the forward motion of the boat on the first torpedo and the subsequent tension on the trigger line. Physical contact with the boat was not necessary to fire the torpedoes because their ignition depended solely on tension on the trigger line. The torpedoes were anchored to the weights and pulleys to ensure pulling of the friction fuse line. It is doubtful that they had any slack line which would allow movement of the torpedo a significant distance before it exploded. Movement of the trigger line about one-half inch could theoretically cause the friction primer to fire. McDaniel's crew did not have enough experience with friction primers to know how to set the trigger lines to account for the effect debris in the river might have if it fouled the trigger lines. With relatively still water and the torpedoes set at a depth of five and a half to six feet, however, moving debris was not much of a problem. Explosive force calculations demonstrate that one torpedo could have caused the damage to the *Cairo*.

A self-detonating electrical torpedo requires a sealed contact switch system in conjunction with the torpedo itself to fire the torpedo. No such switch or system was found. Perry explains the confusion best: "The first Union reports had it that the *Cairo* was a victim of the much discussed 'galvanic torpedoes,' and even experts became confused as to the particular type of explosives used. . . . The torpedoes were held in place by wires stretched from the shore as well, a fact that misled the Federals into assuming that galvanic batteries were located ashore."[61] No galvanic cells were used. But the Union sailors destroyed everything they could see that might have been used by the Confederate torpedo crew. Only a careful examination the next day would tell the Confederates what really happened.

3

We Know She Is at the Bottom

13 December 1862–June 1863

There was no sense in going down to the river at night because nothing could be seen. As Davis, the Confederate torpedo man hiding on a nearby levee, put it, "The Yankees shelled that place till late that day [December 12] so that we did not visit the place until the next day; we had to get our tents and gather up our goods, that we had scattered in the hurry to get out of the way of the shelling; that kept us till night [December 13]; next day [December 14] we went to the place where the boat was sunk, saw the wreck of a boat, drifting on the water."[1]

Ewing, watching from nearby and then withdrawing when the gunfire got intense, wrote in his claim that "the gun boats retired down the river about four o'clock [December 12]. . . . When [Ewing] and several of the men returned to the scene of the wreck [December 13] where we saw a large number of the fragments of the Cairo and her furniture. There was no current in this part of the river and portion of the wreck remained floating on the surface. We had not boat and could not go out to the Cairo that night. The next day [December 14] we procured boats and sounded for and found the wreck."[2]

McDaniel, who was in Vicksburg on the morning of December 12, returned to camp late that evening. Everyone was discussing the recent attack by the Union ships. Curry, Tucker, Dees, and Blake, in their statements prepared in 1864 to support Weldon's claim, all say that no one knew a vessel had been sunk, that McDaniel expressed doubt that the plan "created" by Weldon would work, and that Ewing said he would never have anything to do with torpedoes in the future. Weldon's other witnesses, Beggs and Stancil, make no mention of these allegations, even though Stancil wrote in extremely derogative terms of Ewing and McDaniel. Of course, none of McDaniel's witnesses makes any such statement. If the statements of Curry, Tucker, Dees, and Blake are accurate, then Ewing's is a complete fabrication. There is no explanation of how Ewing had knowledge that could have come only by seeing the *Cairo* hit the mine (e.g., the location of the explosion on the forward port quarter, the anchor chain flying into the air as described by Fentress, and the landing of small boats from the *Pittsburg*). Davis, who was on the levee farther upriver, did not report seeing the ship hit torpedoes but did say he heard a torpedo explode and saw the resulting white smoke.

On December 13, the crew went to the area of their former camp to see what was salvageable. Currie also reported that he "saw on the 13 and 14 inst such signs of the blowing up of a boat as to induce the search."[3] In addition to Currie, at least George Stewart, Isaac Johnston, Charles Brooke, T. O. Davis, Ewing, McDaniel, Edward Blake, and Francis M. Tucker were there.[4] Tucker and Blake mention that Weldon and Lieutenant Francis Shepperd, CSN, were also at the site of the sinking.[5]

Of those at the site, Davis noted:

> At the point where the boat sunk was a shelving bank and that was torn away seamingly [by] the bow of a boat. I saw when they had carried a large cable round a tree, there was a willow top laying fifteen or twenty yards from the bank, and in the Water. I said to the man with me that the boat was on that top, for it was out of sight and proposed that we should sound for it. We got a pole with a spike and hook on the end of it and went out in a short time found the wreck ten or twelve feet under water; and in sounding about found a place and got the hook fast to something; after hard pulling, we brought out a hammock, rolled up right, with a matrass and two blankets in it; after that we got several more and a large chain about seventy yards long.[6]

Brooke reported in his statement for McDaniel that they found "tanks, spittoons, hatches, ladders, portfolio letters and a good many discharges of Illinois Volunteers who had been discharged for the purpose of going on the gun-boat and a great many things that I did not know what they were among the rest was a peace of timber marked Flag Officer Fort Cairo, and a great many large pieces of timber painted black and looked like peaces of a boat."[7]

McDaniel wrote to Governor Pettus about the findings of December 14:

> The gun boats has tried to come up again. They came in contact with a torpedo made to explode by striking & which exploded and tore the boat fearfully. We have been examining the reck and find many peaces of her, some very large ones, but have not as yet found her hull. We know she is at the bottom. The pickets report five boats coming up and but four went down the river. They shelled our camp and blake's lower quarter furiously for several [h]ours. They landed a few men where we had been encamped, but [we] had moved with all our valuable material. The enemy destroyed a few skiffs was the most damage done to us. No one hurt on our side.[8]

Parts of the *Cairo* were later displayed in Governor Pettus's office until the occupation of Jackson, Mississippi, in May 1863, at which time they disappeared.[9]

Some thought was given to removing the guns from the wrecked *Cairo*. Pettus wrote Brown two letters inquiring about the use of the "bell boat." A bell boat was an early form of the diving bell. A bell-shaped device was lowered into the water, and an attached hose and bellows enabled men to work under water for short periods of time. Brown wrote back that he did not think it prudent to open Weldon's obstruction raft just to let the bell boat down to the wreck site. He further noted that if the *Cairo* was damaged, as he believed, with only the hull stove in and settled on the bottom, the intact iron roof would prevent removal of the guns. He confirmed the "total destruction of the boat and probably every one on board, though it is hard to believe that among so many Yankees there should not have been a few born to be hanged."[10]

In the Christmas Day edition of the *New York Times*, the paper's special correspondent reported the sinking of the *Cairo*. He attributed the torpedoes to "a man named Ivins—originally a native of the state in whose metropolis revolves the Hub of the Universe." He described the torpedo as

> a common twelve-gallon demijohn . . . filled . . . with powder and sat it upon the end of a log of wood some three feet in length. To the lower end of this log was fastened an iron staple, in which was tied the end of a piece of

strong rope. An anchor attached to this rope held the log under water, while the other end of the rope, after being passed through the eye of the anchor, was fastened to a stump ashore. In the neck of the demijohn was placed some fulminating powder, the end of a wire well roughened was inserted in this, the whole well-waxed to keep it water-tight, and then the balance of this wire was extended just below the surface of the river and fastened to something on the bank."[11]

Also on Christmas Day 1862, Isaac Brown wrote to Mallory:

I had the honor recently to send to the Department, two telegrams regarding the torpedo destroyed gunboat of the enemy in the lower Yazoo. No doubt now exists but that the destruction was complete and instantaneous involving perhaps the loss of every one on board. The boat seems to have been either the "Cairo" or the "Cincinnati", both of which were ironclads of 13 guns. At the moment of its destruction, it was with four others ascending the Yazoo and shelling the banks to drive back our pickets—and intending no doubt to attack our defenses at Snyder's Mills from which they were still about four miles distand. The four boats returned from the point of the explosion with it is reported the black flag flying. They have not since been seen in the Yazoo. I had before hearing of the success of Acting Masters McDaniel and Ewing send at the request of Maj. Gen. M. L. Smith, 1st Lt. F. E. Shepperd, to investigate the proceedings and some days before that time I had sent acting Gunner Burton, CSN, to the assistance of the torpedo party. Though full credit must be given Acting Masters McDaniel and Ewing for their success, I think that they were probably fortunate in obtaining Mr. Burton's aid as probably their immediate success was owing to a suggestion of his to use "friction primers" instead of their method of setting off the torpedoes.

Credit in this connection is also due Mr. Thomas Weldon, builder of the raft at Snyder's Mills and contractor for the gun boat, at this place for zeal and energy in procuring materials for the torpedo party. But this does not take from the merits of Messrs. McDaniel and Ewing for long persistance in their plans under rather discouraging local circumstances. Every assistance asked for by those gentlemen shall be cheerfully given on my part, as has heretofore been done—and when the enemy again attempt to ascend the Yazoo casualties, sudden and severe, may perhaps overtake them—I submit herewith on a separate paper, a written description of the torpedo so used in the destruction of the enemy's boat.[12]

Death was to be the lot of the next Union flotilla to ascend the Yazoo, but that moment belonged to Edward Higgins's artillery, Weldon's barrier, and McDaniel's torpedo corps. On December 23, 1862, a second flotilla, in preparation for Sherman's assault at Chickasaw Bayou, ascended the Yazoo River to the vicinity of the *Cairo* wreck and began sweeping for torpedoes.[13] In that flotilla were the *Benton*, *Queen of the West*, *Signal*, another Eads ironclad, *Baron de Kalb*, and a tug. Lieutenant William Gwinn of the *Benton* was in command. By December 24, the boats had moved upriver to the vicinity of Weldon's obstruction raft, now covered by the newly developed friction-primer-fired torpedoes. The Confederate batteries on Haynes' Bluff, consisting of fourteen rifled guns of 7.5-inch, 8-inch, and 10-inch size, were manned by Company A, First Mississippi Artillery, and Cowan's Battery. Infantry support was provided by the Twenty-second Louisiana Regiment and the Third Mississippi Regiment. The Confederates opened a severe cannonade on the small flotilla, mangling the *Benton*, killing Lieutenant Gwinn, and forcing the boats to withdraw without opening the Yazoo north of Snyder's Bluff.

On December 27, 1862, General William T. Sherman's long-awaited assault on Vicksburg began through Chickasaw Bayou. By January 2, 1863, Sherman had accomplished nothing but suffered more than seventeen hundred casualties trying to negotiate the swamps of the bayou and making a frontal assault on the bluffs of Walnut Hills. Sherman, hearing that Major General John A. McClernand had arrived from Illinois and was at the mouth of the Yazoo, withdrew his forces and turned over his command to McClernand. Sherman learned from McClernand that Grant's depot at Holly Springs had been destroyed by a Confederate raid and Grant would not be coming to assist in the assault on Vicksburg. Sherman's losses were for nothing.

Several persons now knew how to construct torpedoes, including Burton and Weldon. It was time for Zere McDaniel to move on to other locations, where his expertise and his torpedoes could be used to help the cause. On January 5, 1863, Zere McDaniel left Vicksburg and the Yazoo River, never to return.[14] He decided, for reasons unknown today, to continue torpedo operations in other areas on the Mississippi River and in Louisiana. He was accompanied by John Beggs, who stated that he was with McDaniel from November 11, 1862, until April 27, 1863.[15] McDaniel never mentioned who he was with from January 1863 until his arrival in Richmond in July. The statements of D. M. Currie, T. O. Davis, Stewart, Johnston, and Brooke that were included in McDaniel's later claim were obtained in Jackson, Mississippi, probably by Ewing, between February 10 and 25, 1863. Some or all of these men may have traveled with him in January.

McDaniel's first stop was at Port Hudson, Louisiana, 120 miles south of

Vicksburg, and the last remaining bastion of Confederate strength on the Mississippi besides Vicksburg. During the first week of January 1863, General Pemberton sent General John Gregg's infantry brigade and a field artillery battery by steamboat from Vicksburg to Port Hudson.[16] McDaniel and those with him may have gotten a ride on this voyage.

Port Hudson was slowly being invested by Union army and navy forces, as was Vicksburg. Like Vicksburg, its towering bluffs overlooking the Mississippi gave it command of the river, causing great risk to the Union navy in attempting to pass its guns. By January 1863, most Confederate strategists believed that the Union forces would try to take Port Hudson by assault from the land side and that similar tactics would be tried against Vicksburg. If both positions held on, however, the Confederacy would still control the river and enormous numbers of Union troops would be tied up, unable to support Union operations then in progress in Tennessee.

Following the end of fighting in Kentucky, Union Major General Don Carlos Buell was relieved by Major General William S. Rosecrans as commander of the Army of the Cumberland. Opposite this force were three Confederate corps of General Braxton Bragg's Army of Tennessee. Rosecrans occupied the city of Nashville and then spent several months preparing for his invasion across Tennessee to Georgia in an effort to cut the Confederacy in half. On December 26, 1862, Rosecrans began his advance against the Confederate lines. The Confederate right was anchored at Readyville, Tennessee, and occupied by Major General John McCown's corps. The Confederate center was at Murfreesboro, Tennessee, occupied by Lieutenant General Leonidas K. Polk. The left wing of Bragg's army was firmly entrenched at Triune and Eagleville, Tennessee, under Lieutenant General W. J. Hardee. To meet the Union onslaught, Bragg withdrew his wings and concentrated his forces at Murfreesboro.

While Confederate cavalry surveilled his movements and harassed his exterior lines, Rosecrans took an overly cautious four days to advance the twenty miles over first-class road to Murfreesboro. At dawn on December 31, the Confederates initiated an assault against the Union lines. Fierce seesaw battles ensued in the area around Murfreesboro and Stone's River. Some units on both sides lost upward of 40 percent of their effective strength in killed, wounded, or prisoners. By January 4, 1863, both sides had been seriously bloodied, each losing about 26 percent of its total combat strength. Finally, on the morning of January 4, Bragg retired his forces from the field, using General Joseph Wheeler's cavalry to screen his withdrawal until January 5. Bragg's army fell back to a position near Shelbyville, Tennessee.

Confederate intelligence collection and torpedo operations continued at Port Hudson in the early months of 1863. Ewing reported in his claim that he and McDaniel had developed a new mode of riverine warfare for torpedoes:

> Their man of war is simply a hollowed log with the natural interior—a cavity within of sufficient length and diameter to conceal one man at its bow and another at its stern.—A small hole for observations in front and rear and a rudder attached and submerged at the stern to enable a hand to direct its course upon the enemys vessel. The water fills the log to the level of the river but there remains a sufficient air chamber above the water in the log to sustaine life for several hours. Experiments have proven that a log-boat thus arranged will not turn over in the water, but maintain its position like other boats. The torpedo is submerged from five to six feet below another log acting as a float. A line is attached to the end of the float log and another to the friction primer inserted in the [neck] of the torpedo. Those lines are wound upon a reel which is held by the men in the log-boat and the torpedo is thus drawn after them until it is brought in contact with the enemys vessel. The liens are then paid out from the reel until the log boat floats a safe distance from the torpedo when by sudden jerk of the line attached to the friction primer in the torpedo and explosion is produced and the enemys vessel is destroyed. . . . We made preparations to fight the enemys gun boat Essex in daylight at Vicksburg when she was last there, but were prevented by orders to the contrary. We are now willing to fight the Essex or any other gunboat at Port Hudson or elsewhere. . . . Your petitioners have already passed through the enemys fleet in this matter when below Vicksburg—touched one of their gunboats overheard conversation on board—then floated off with the current, landed at a safe distance below and returned unharmed to the city.[17]

At Port Hudson, according to historian Lawrence L. Hewitt, a "select group of Confederate officers and men formed a special detail that constructed rafts and torpedoes. The rafts might obstruct passage of enemy vessels, but the torpedoes had a more deadly purpose—the destruction of a vessel, especially the *Essex*."[18] The USS *Essex* was a target at Port Hudson as well as at Vicksburg. On Monday, January 19, 1863, Port Hudson diarist Robert Patrick reported: "The old 'Essex' is lying down below and fired some guns this morning at something. A plan is being laid to blow her up with something like a submarine battery as soon as they can have it fixed up. I am afraid that it will not succeed although this same man who is contriving this, managed to destroy two other boats up the Yazoo River and if he has been successful before, I do not see why he should not be able to accomplish the same feat here that he did there".[19]

Another report of Confederate torpedo activity protecting Port Hudson came on January 16, 1863, from John Wesley Powers, Company H, First Alabama Regiment: "It appears that they are afraid to make the venture, since one of their best Boats were blown up at or near the mouth of the Yazoo, by one of Mr. Stewarts Torpedoes. There are some of the same kind of articles now in the River about six miles below here. So if they undertake to come up with their Boats they will be apt to strike some of them, and if they do, they will be apt to be Blown up." Hewitt also reported that "an unusual floating torpedo was attached to a log. Adding a cotton bale to attract the enemy's attention, the Confederates released the disguised bomb and allowed it to drift downstream."[20] But a Negro alerted the crew of the *Essex* to the torpedo attempt, and the crew of the ship foiled the plan. Several attempts were made over the next few months, but each failed to damage the *Essex*.[21]

McDaniel reported that he remained at Port Hudson only until some time in February 1863.[22] He and Beggs then traveled to Baton Rouge, Louisiana, to attempt further torpedo operations there. It is possible that Currie, Davis, Stewart, Johnston, and Brooke, all of whom were Mississippians, decided to remain in Mississippi instead of following McDaniel to his next location, Baton Rouge, Louisiana. Ewing left McDaniel at this point, gathered statements in support of his and McDaniel's claim, and proceeded to Richmond.

Although Baton Rouge was captured by Union forces early in the war because of the presence of a Federal armory there, it was the site of a battle in August 1862. On August 21, Union forces abandoned Baton Rouge.[23] In November 1862, General Nathaniel P. Banks relieved General Benjamin F. Butler as commander of the Department of the Gulf and was ordered to open up the Mississippi. One of his first moves was to garrison Baton Rouge with ten thousand troops. Nothing is known of McDaniel's efforts at Baton Rouge except for his statement to Jefferson Davis that he "made an uncucessful [sic] 'lick' at the enemys vessels."[24]

McDaniel's next stop was at Franklin, Louisiana, arriving in Late February or early April 1863. He reported his actions: "I went to Franklin, La., and there established shops to make rope, life preservers & torpedoes. While there at the request of Gen Richard Taylor I placed a number of submarine batteries in the Bayou Teche; which detered the enemies Gun Boats and held them off when Gen Taylor had to retreat; and I am satisfied saved the army from capture."[25]

In early April 1863, Banks began the Red River Campaign. He was unwilling to risk assaulting the Confederate garrison at strongly defended Port Hudson until he secured the west bank of the Mississippi River. To do this, he needed to neutralize Taylor's forces, which were concentrated near Franklin, Louisiana. Banks ordered Brigadier General Cuvier Grover's division from Baton Rouge, Brigadier General William H. Emory's division, and Brigadier General Godfrey Weitzel's brigade from New Orleans and directed them to converge on Brashear City (now Morgan City), Louisiana.

Between April 12 and 14, 1863, a series of sharp engagements were fought between Taylor's Confederates and Banks's forces in a small strip of land between Brashear City and New Iberia. The topography aided Taylor's defense. His left flank was on Grand Lake, a major body of water. His right flank anchored on Bayou Teche, a navigable waterway running northwest to southeast through the Louisiana delta. Further to support his approximately five thousand men, Taylor positioned the captured Union ram *Queen of the West* in Grand Lake and the gunboat CSS *Diana* in Bayou Teche.

The *Diana* was a side-wheel steamer of 239 tons, mounting five guns. She was seized by Union naval forces in April 1862 at New Orleans and recaptured by Confederate forces on Bayou Teche, near Pattersonville, Louisiana, on March 28, 1863. She was to provide gunfire support to Taylor's withdrawal from Fort Bisland, but before she could be used, she was burned to avoid capture on April 12.

The Union plan of attack was to send Grover's division up Grand Lake to cut off Taylor's line of retreat at Irish Bend. Collaterally, Emory and Weitzel would attack Taylor head-on at Fort Bisland to keep the Confederates from retreating before Grover's envelopment took place. The *Queen of the West* was the same ram that McDaniel had faced on December 12, 1862, in the Yazoo. She was raised by the Confederates following her sinking by the guns at Fort DeRussy, Louisiana, on February 14, 1863. Her purpose on Grand Lake was to prevent just such an envelopment of Taylor as Grover planned.

Emory and Weitzel attacked Taylor in the early afternoon hours of April 12. Fighting continued throughout the afternoon. On April 13, Emory and Weitzel continued their pressure with superior forces and by nightfall came to within four hundred yards of Fort Bisland's parapets. Unknown to Emory and Weitzel, Grover suffered a series of delays caused by failure to reconnoiter his route. One of his gunboats, the USS *Arizona*, grounded, his debarkation was delayed for lack of adequate roads inland from Grand Lake, and his boats could approach no nearer to the shore than one hundred yards.

On the morning of April 14, the Federal forces renewed their assault on Fort Bisland only to find that the Confederates had evacuated the fort during the night and begun their withdrawal northward along the Teche. Taylor, now well north of his former position, ran into Grover's undeployed troops. After a sharp skirmish, Taylor extricated himself from the intended trap and moved northward. He retreated successively through New Iberia, Vermillionville, and Opelousas. Also on April 14, the *Queen of the West* was attacked by the *Arizona*, the *Estrella*, and the *Calhoun* on the Atchafalaya River, a feeder tributary for Grand Lake. A shot from the *Calhoun*, a captured Confederate privateer, set her cotton bale siding on fire and she exploded.

McDaniel reported later to Jefferson Davis, "in this fight, being in the rear with my batteries, while the army was getting away. And having no horses to hall away my tools and materials, I lost evry thing but six locks."[26] McDaniel was caught up in the fast retreat of Taylor's forces on the fourteenth. By April 17, McDaniel made his way to Alexandria, Louisiana, sixty miles north of Opelousas, with the retreating Confederate forces. At Alexandria, he applied for and received $621 from the post quartermaster, Major T. R. Heard, for "amount expended for submarine purposes."[27]

During his tour in Louisiana, McDaniel served under the command of General Henry Gray.[28] Gray, a Confederate congressman when he was commissioned, served as the commanding officer (colonel) of the Twenty-eighth Louisiana Regiment under Taylor. Although wounded in the Teche battle, on April 15, 1863, he was given a field promotion to brigadier general by General E. Kirby Smith and put in command of a brigade in Brigadier General Alfred Mouton's division.[29] Like many of McDaniel's connections, this one would serve him in the future.

We do not know exactly when McDaniel left Louisiana and how he traveled from Alexandria to the vicinity of Tullahoma, Tennessee, but he must have left soon after April 18. General Banks occupied Alexandria on May 7 with little opposition.

In April 1863, the two routes from Alexandria, Louisiana, east to Mississippi were along interior roads of questionable passability or via boat along the Red River to the Mississippi. There were no rail lines in the area. Confederates still held Fort DeRussy on the Red River. The most likely route was by boat along the Red River to Port Hudson or Vicksburg. On April 15, Grant began the naval portion of his operation, which would result ultimately in the capture of Vicksburg. The Union fleet made a run past the guns at Vicksburg on April 15, arriving at Carthage. By May 3, Grant landed troops at Grand Gulf and prepared to move inland toward Raymond. Because the mouth of the Red River was a few miles north of Port Hudson and Banks was moving north, up the Teche and Atchafalaya, behind him, McDaniel most likely chose to go by boat from Alexandria to Port Hudson. From Port Hudson, he would have to travel part of the way to Tullahoma by horseback.[30] He had $621 so he could have purchased a horse. Beggs stated that he and McDaniel parted company on April 27, which was about the time McDaniel left Port Hudson.[31]

Major General William S. Rosecrans spent the six months from January to June 1863 resting and refitting his mauled Army of the Cumberland after the battles at Murfreesboro and Stone's River. Finally, in June he decided to proceed with his campaign. Bragg, alerted to Rosecrans's movement, initially decided to offer battle at Shelbyville, Tennessee, but following the turning of his left flank, withdrew to Tullahoma. On the morning of June 24, Union forces began to exert pressure against the Confederate flanks and continued that pressure through the twenty-seventh. That day, the major body of Confederate troops withdrew to Tullahoma and established positions there. At this critical moment, Bragg's health failed and his corps commanders advised him to retreat. Rather than risk a battle in ill health, and after several serious reversals on the field, Bragg on June 27 ordered the Army of Tennessee to withdraw from Tullahoma and move toward Chattanooga. The Confederates reached that city on July 7. Vicksburg had surrendered on July 4 and Port Hudson would surrender on July 9.

McDaniel probably arrived at Bragg's position sometime in May or early June 1863. All of his known prior experience was with explosive devices under water. Now he faced a new challenge—working with explosives on dry land. McDaniel wrote to Davis that after he left Alexandria, he "went to Gen Braggs army where by his authority, I have been inventing and operating a method to destroy the trains of the enemy on the Rail Roads. And, just before the retreat from Tullahoma [June 27, 1863], I destroyed two heavy laden trains between Nashville and Murfresborow. Making total wrecks of them according to the enemys own account."[32] He rapidly adapted to the need and developed explosive devices capable of being used against railroads. To destroy two trains in the location he identified, McDaniel or the sabotage crew would have had to go behind enemy lines because the area between Nashville and Murfreesboro was occupied by Union troops.

Working with explosives on dry land eliminated the major problem McDaniel had encountered on the Yazoo—water. Too, when explosives are planted in solid earth, the earth below directs the explosive force upward, unlike water, in which the force of the explosion expands as shock waves equally in all directions. Ideally, railroad torpedoes would be placed in a curve at the bottom of a grade on the outside rail. Following the destruction of the locomotive and its derailment, the momentum of the rest of the train would result in total destruction. The triggering device would be a hook from the friction primer arranged to catch on the cowcatcher of the locomotive. A pull on the wire would detonate the charge, preferably just ahead of the locomotive. A wire of the required size was invisible to the crew of the moving train.[33]

It was typical of McDaniel not to put any detail in his letter to Davis because, as he said, he was "inventing" a method to operate against railroads. McDaniel was always alert to the possibility of receiving reward for his work. To put sensitive proprietary data in a letter that might be read by others was not his style. Now, with experience on water and land, he was ready for whatever opportunity crossed his path.

4

Form a Company of Men for Secret Service

July 1863–December 1863

On March 23, 1863, McDaniel and Ewing, in a statement prepared by Ewing, who was in Richmond, made a claim on the Confederate government based on a "secret" act of the Confederate Congress, which entitled persons who destroyed material of the enemy, using an original invention, to one-half the value of the material destroyed. That act was an amendment to an original act. The pertinent part was as follows: "In case any person or persons shall invent or construct any new machine or engine or construct any new method of destroying the armed vessels of the enemy he or they shall receive *fifty percentum* of the value of each and every such vessel that may be sunk or destroyed by means of such invention or contrivance, including the value of the armament thereof in lieu of the twenty percentum as provided by said act." The previous act also provided for "the valuation to be made by a board of Naval Officers, appointed and their award to be approved by the President, and the amount found due to be payable in eight percent bonds of the Confederate states."[1]

McDaniel and Ewing made their claim based on the torpedo used to sink the *Cairo*. In support of their claim, they included the statements of

USS *Cairo* (Courtesy Library of Congress)

USS *Marmora* (Courtesy Library of Congress)

USS *Signal* (Courtesy Library of Congress)

USS *Pittsburg* (Courtesy Library of Congress)

USS *Queen of the West* ([c] Tony Gibbons courtesy of Bernard Thornton Artists. London, UK. *Warships and Battles of the Civil War,* 1989)

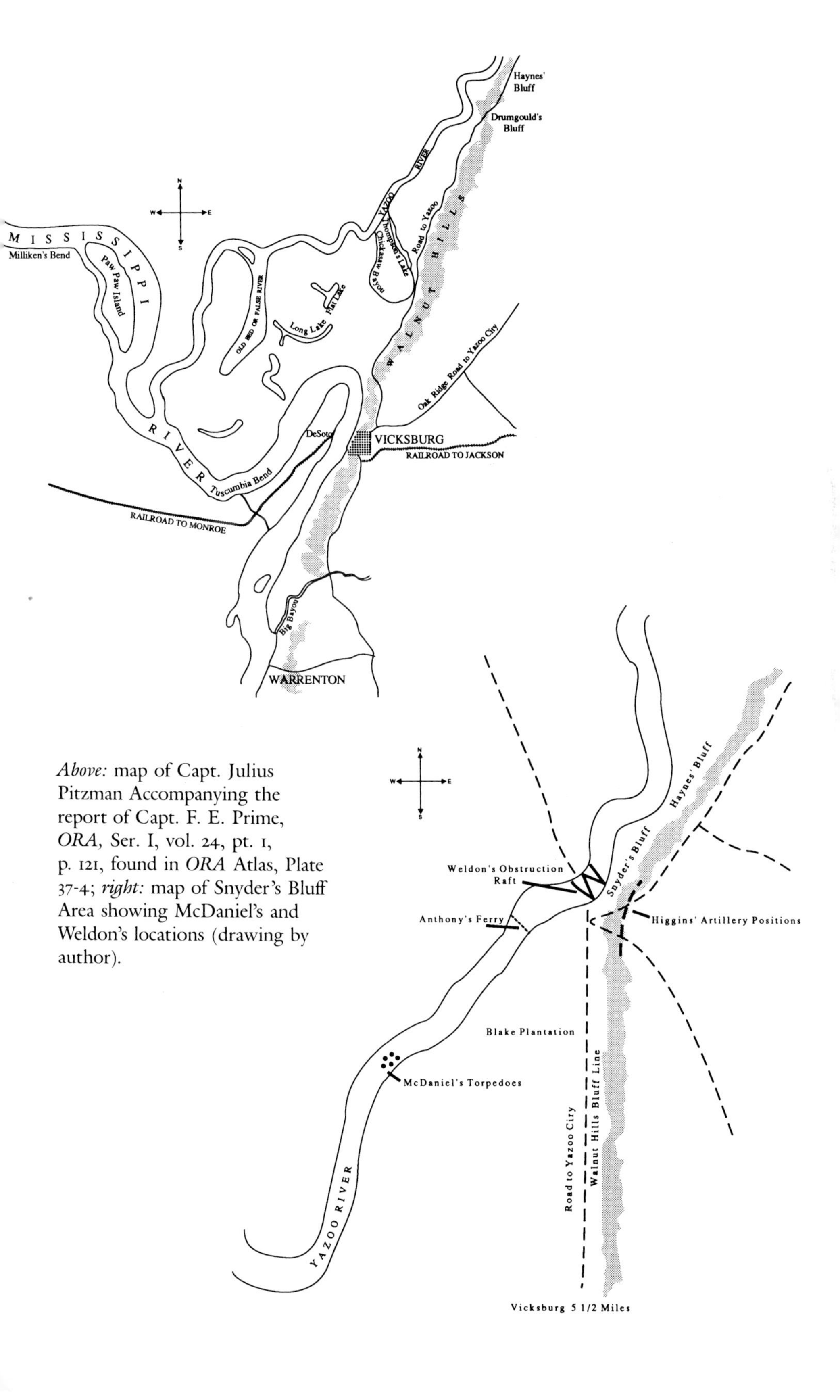

Above: map of Capt. Julius Pitzman Accompanying the report of Capt. F. E. Prime, *ORA,* Ser. I, vol. 24, pt. 1, p. 121, found in *ORA* Atlas, Plate 37-4; *right:* map of Snyder's Bluff Area showing McDaniel's and Weldon's locations (drawing by author).

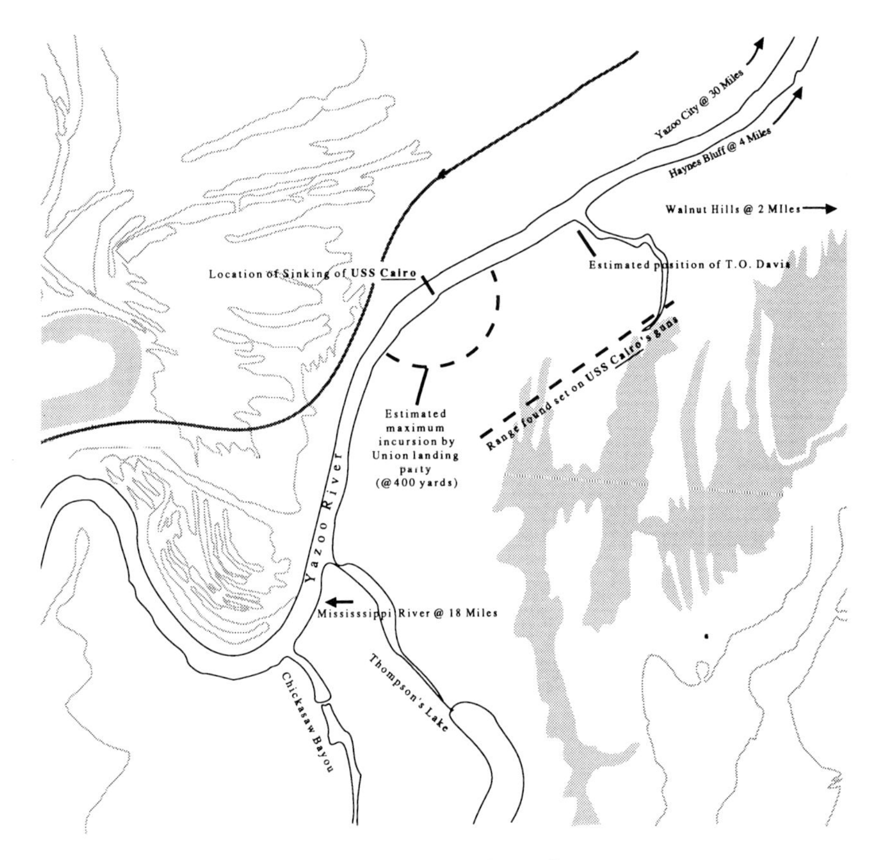

Yazoo river at *Cairo* combat area (annotated by author)

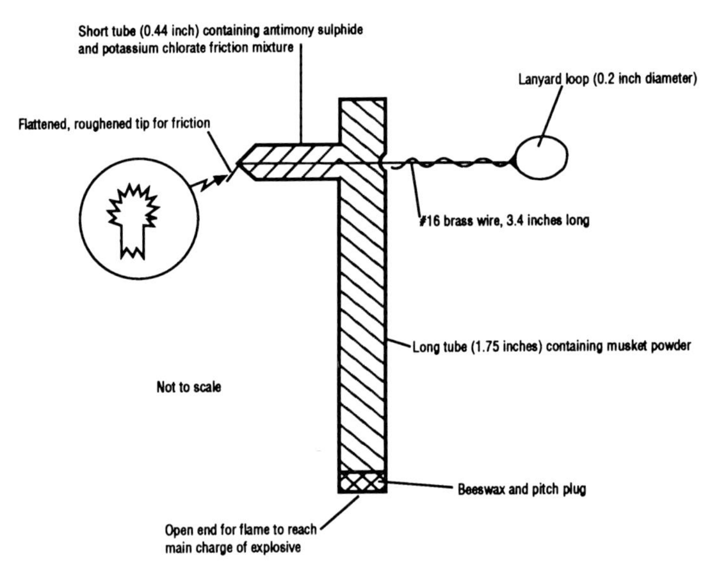

Cutaway view of U.S. military friction primer c. 1862 (drawing by author)

Ammunition wharf at City Point, Virginia, in 1864 before explosion (Courtesy Library of Congress)

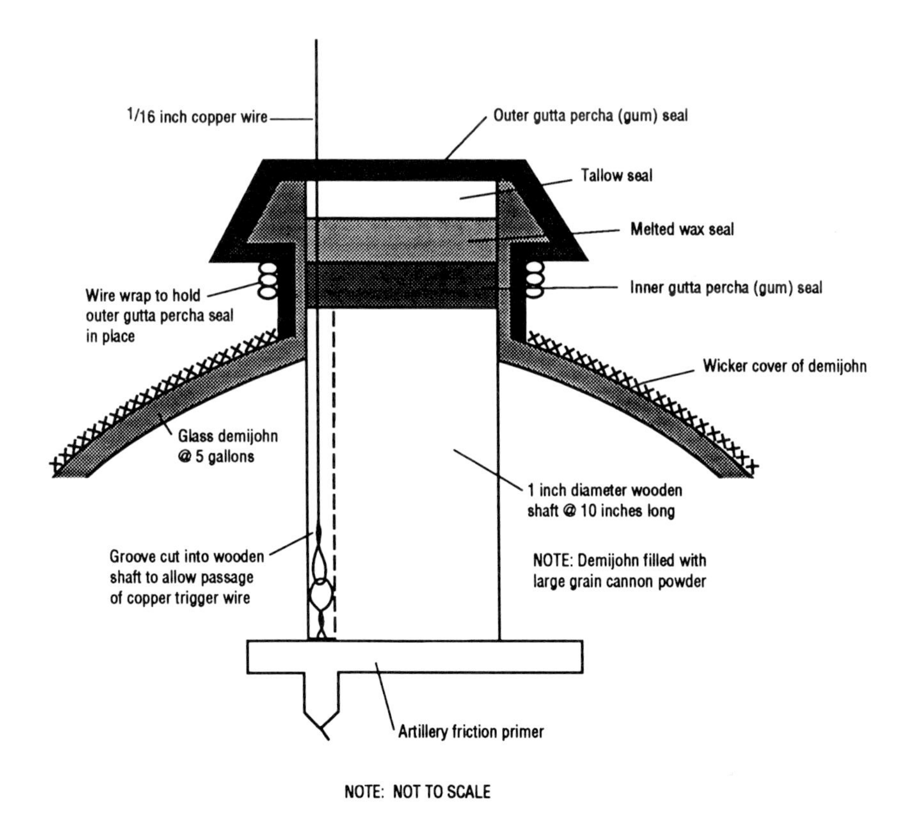

Drawing of the torpedo used to sink the *Cairo* as described by David Curry and others (drawing by author)

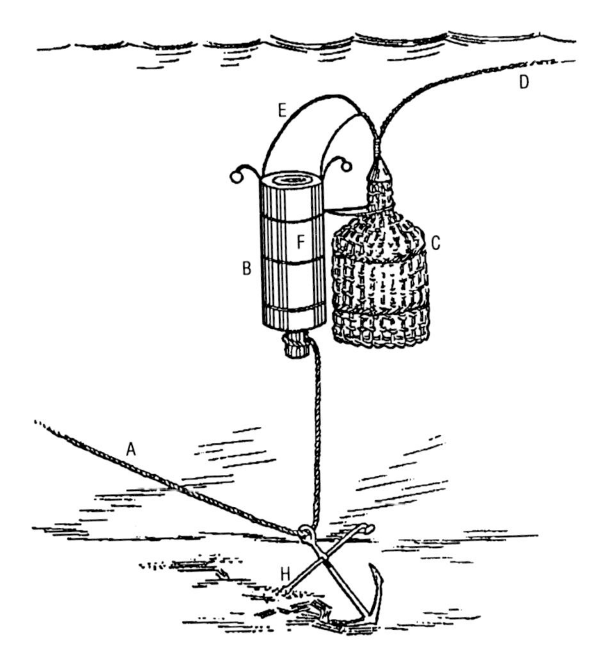

Fentress's drawing of the torpedo found in the Yazoo (*ORN,* Ser. I, vol. 25, p. 549)

Above and left: mid-nineteenth-century wicker-covered five-gallon glass demijohn (Courtesy Glenwood Foundation, Charleston, West Virginia) (photographs by author)

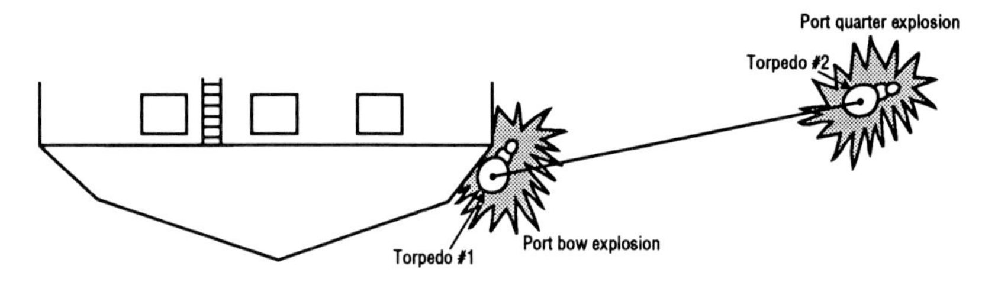

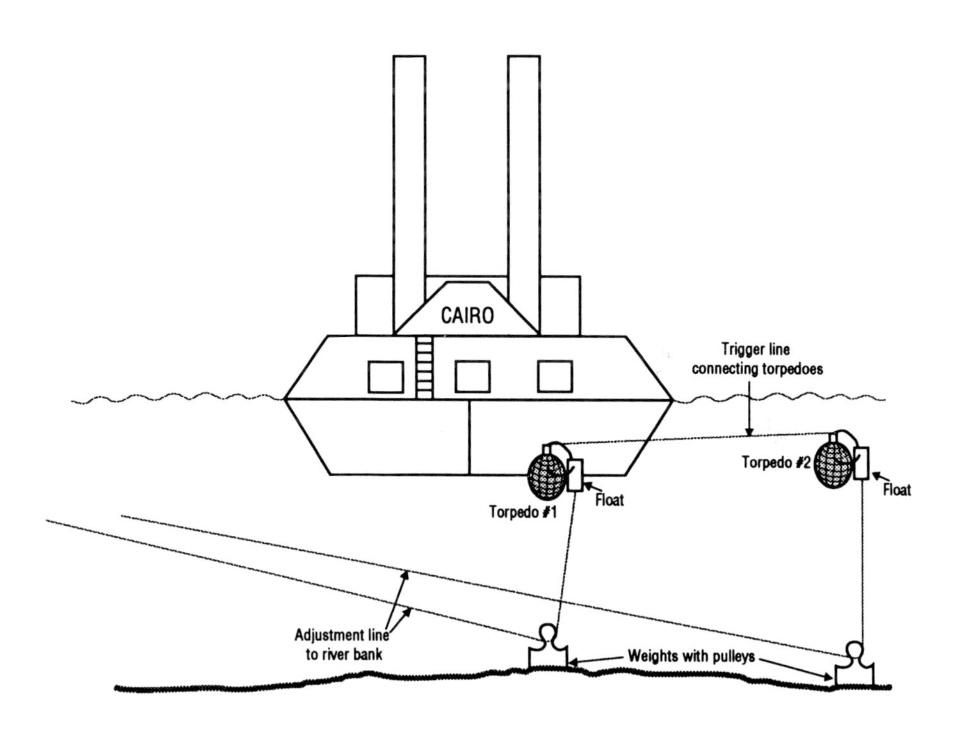

Drawing of how the *Cairo* probably struck Confederate torpedoes (drawing by author)

Torpedo damage to forward port hull

Above: close-up view of forward port quarter of hull showing area of torpedo damage; *right:* side view of forward port quarter showing torpedo damage area directly under forward port cannon.

Photographs of the Cairo *today showing torpedo damage to forward port bow area (photographs by author)*

A. Lacy,[2] Currie, Stewart, Johnston, Brooke, and Davis. They also used the December 25, 1862, letter of Brown to Secretary Mallory. They claimed that they invented the torpedo in the spring or early summer of 1862 in Mississippi. Following its invention, it was tested and tried on the Yazoo and ultimately resulted in the destruction of the *Cairo*. In accordance with the law, the claim was initially sent to Jefferson Davis.

It is probable that McDaniel and Ewing knew of the secret act provisions before the sinking of the *Cairo*. In August 1863, Secretary of War James A. Seddon sent a letter to General E. Kirby Smith advising him of the pending arrival of seven men to be "employed in your department on the special service of destroying the enemy's property by torpedoes and similar inventions." He directed that "these men should each be enlisted in and form part of an engineer company" and that "their compensation will be 50 percent of the property destroyed by them by the use of torpedoes or similar devices. Beyond this, they will be entitled to such other reward as Congress may here after provide." Seddon wrote a similar letter to General Joseph E. Johnston, commanding the Department of the West, listing the names of nine persons to be so employed with Johnston, including two of the Confederacy's leading torpedo experts, E. C. Singer, a Texas gunsmith who was related to the inventor of the sewing machine, and J. R. Fretwell.[3]

Davis forwarded the McDaniel-Ewing claim to Secretary of the Navy Mallory for his comments. McDaniel and Ewing were represented in their claim by General John D. Freeman, an attorney in Richmond. Freeman, anticipating approval of the claim, located a Confederate naval officer with prior U.S. Navy experience, Sydney H. McAddam, and sent a series of interrogatories to him concerning the *Cairo*. McAddam detailed his knowledge of the *Cairo*'s construction, listing her armament, crew size, and construction size:

> My name is Sydney Hugh McAddam, am thirty-four years of age, have followed the occupation of sailor for twenty years—thirteen of which time have been spent in the public service—the remaining years in that of the United States. Was appointed to the Confederate States Gunboat "W. H. Webb" the 30th day of December 1862 by Brig. Genl. Blanchard (as per copy of Report) at Monroe, La., and ordered by him now to report to the Secretary of War, for transfer from the War to the Navy Department.
>
> My experience respecting the building of vessels of war have been both extensive and varied, and in the construction of gunboats, large, having been in the service of the United States at the outbreak of the war, on duty

under Capt. A. H. Foote, U.S.N., in charge of construction of gunboats at that place. Consider myself capable of laying the keel of a ship and superintending her construction as well as though I was practically in that business.

I have a personal knowledge of United States Gunboat "Cairo" mentioned in this interrogatory. The "Cairo" was built at Mound City, Illinois, by Messrs Rodes and Nilson, was commenced in June 1861 and put in commission in January 1862, her length over all was 185 feet, breadth of beam 53 feet, depth of hull 7 feet—1 built flat bottomed and without a keel—her frame was ten inch oak timber, 24 inches from center to center to the angle of her sides or the foot of her case mate. her casemate frames were 8 inch oak timber thirty inches from center to center, her planking was four inch oak and her lining six inch—she had a rail running around her, her angle of one foot oak square oak bolted through and [nutted] inside, her iron plating consisted of two and a half inch iron plates ten inches wide, and the entire length of her sides from her angle to her spar deck—she had an angular case mate forward, and one aft, composed of twenty-four inch solid oak, with 2-1/2 inch iron plating outside. Her deck, well laid of four inch pink plank, on ten inch [Carlines] or beams. Her mail cladding was composed together of two and a half inch iron bolted from outside and countersunk in the plating and nutted inside. Her boilers, 4 in number were in her hold, and covered with an additional casemate, built angularly and twenty or twenty-four inches thick while her engines were composed of two high pressure engines of thirty inch cylinders and ten feet stroke with a "Ductor" for supplying ship and boiler with water. Hot water hose, two in number, on each side led from the after end of her boilers the extreme length of her decks to be used as a protection against boarders. She had one paddle wheel, between her engines, and in the centre of the boat pretty well aft and was considered their fastest boat a year ago.

Her armament consisted of 3–7 inch rifle guns forward, or what in the old service used to be called—42 pdr sea coast howitzers which have since been rifled out. These guns carrying a shell weighing 80 or 85 pounds. Her two forward broadside guns were 8 inch smoothbore guns (64 pds) the remaining part of her broadsides being filled up with medium 32s smoothbore. Her stern guns, 2 in number, one being situated in the cabin the others in the ward room, were 50 pdr Parrott guns, and on her spar deck, she carried 2—12 pdr Dahlgren Howitzers, smoothbores.

Her small arms consisted of Colts revolvers, cutlasses and boarding pikes disposed of as is usual on board ship to gun crews. Her crew numbered about one hundred eighty men composed of a commander, 4 masters, 2 masters mates, 2 pilots with rank of Lieut., Pursers, surgeon and the usual number of petty officers as on board a 3rd class man of war. to which class she belonged. She was commanded at the time of her sinking, by Lieut. Comdg Thos. A. Selfridge formerly executive officer of the "Cumberland". He having been on board of her at the time of the attack made on that ves-

> sel by the Confederate Gunboat "Merrimac" off Fort Monroe last Summer.
>
> I know the amount of her cost to the Federal government, at the time of her build, exclusive of her armament, stores, etc, her cost was two hundred and eighty thousand dollars which was considered amounting to one half her entire value, when fully equipped and manned with guns and stores on board.
>
> She had sharpshooters on board, arrived with Enfield Rifles, but disposed of as only Naval officers know of, when in action, their number can only be accurately ascertained by calculating the GunCrews and small arms men in the powder and shell division. I have no way of ascertaining their value.[4]

Within forty-five days, Freeman had his reply from Secretary Mallory. Mallory was going to recommend that President Davis deny the claim because McDaniel and Ewing were naval officers on duty at the time of the sinking of the *Cairo*. He admitted that "the terms of the . . . act seem to be broad and comprehensive enough to embrace all who those [sic] destroy an enemys ship of war, salaried officers of the government included! but I think their proper construction can only be arrived at by considering them in connection with the terms used in the two previous acts . . . and a fair construction in my judgment excludes the claim here presented." Three days later, Mallory wrote to Davis, enclosing a copy of his letter to Freeman and a copy of a legal brief by Freeman, recommending that Davis deny the claim. In a concise note at the bottom of Mallory's letter, dated May 23, 1863, Davis dismissed the claim: "The argument of counsel submitted by you maintains ably that a public officer or employee may be a patentee but I do not perceive that this was denied, the question being whether the Govt should pay its naval officers for the destruction of an enemys vessel by a new contrivance, invention or otherwise construing the laws relating to the subjects as a whole. Your conclusion seems to me correct. The papers are returned."[5] Freeman, not to be outdone, sought and received an opinion from Confederate Attorney General F. H. Watts which fully supported McDaniel and Ewing's claim.

McDaniel arrived in Richmond sometime during the first two weeks of July 1863.[6] His and Ewing's claim had been denied by Davis and Mallory on May 19 in Mallory's letter to General Freeman.[7] McDaniel contacted George Work, who provided a statement, dated July 17 at Richmond, to accompany McDaniel's written plea to Davis to reconsider of July 18. Work reported that he left Jackson, Mississippi, on June 30, apparently making the trip to Richmond in about two weeks.[8]

In his long letter to Davis, McDaniel detailed his life history to that point, including his operations at Port Hudson, Franklin (with General Richard Taylor), and Tullahoma (with General Braxton Bragg) and further described the hardships of life in the torpedo corps. He also argued the legal aspects of the matter, explaining why he was appointed an acting master in the navy. In addition, he submitted the statement from George Work and another from Senator John B. Clark of Missouri.[9] McDaniel emphasized that Watts's opinion was that it did not matter whether McDaniel and Ewing were in the navy but that the act of Congress permitted an interpretation which included naval personnel.

Using his network of allies, McDaniel summoned other political figures to his cause. H. W. Bruce, a staunch supporter of the president and McDaniel's representative from Kentucky, resubmitted the claim to Davis on July 20, 1863, drawing particular attention to Watts's opinion.[10] Davis, as usual, forwarded Bruce's submission to Mallory with an endorsement: "Attorney General for advice." Mallory now began to feel the political heat of the situation. He wrote: "The case presented in the supplemental statement of McDaniel and Ewing recommends it strongly to careful consideration, but the grounds upon [which] its rejection was placed still remain; and with every desire to see the service performed by these gentlemen properly rewarded and encouragement given thereby to others to labour in the same field, this Department deems itself powerless to grant as prayed." Mallory prepared an extensive report which included an opinion of the attorney general on a prior, unrelated matter. This opinion supported Mallory's contention that the amendment under which McDaniel and Ewing's claim was made was unconstitutional because it failed to state properly the contents in the title.[11]

McDaniel and Ewing, determined to see the matter through, wrote an open letter to the Confederate Congress requesting that body to validate their claim and force Davis to pay it.[12] Their letter was referred to the Committee of Naval Affairs of the Confederate Senate. On January 6, 1864, the committee reviewed the history of the claim, the legal arguments about the title of the act, and the claimants' naval status and in its findings blasted Mallory for daring to challenge a legislative function:

> The constitutional objection is one we doubt the right of an executive officer to raise. If Congress passes and the President approves an act, it does not belong to a Secretary to oppose its execution, on the ground that it is unconstitutional. But the ground taken is more technical than solid. . . . It

could never have been meant by the framers of the Constitution that executive officers should refuse to obey laws, simply because Congress had not, in their judgment, with sufficient clearness expressed in the title what was the subject of the law. We prefer to allow Congress to propose, and the President to approve, not only the laws themselves, but the titles; and this being done, we think executive officers are estopped."[13]

Following the Senate committee's finding, the Senate, also on January 6, proposed a joint resolution, Senate Resolution 22, for the benefit of McDaniel and Ewing. The resolution stated that the two men "are entitled to the benefits of an act approved April 21st, 1862," and "this without reference to the questions, as to whether the subject, of said act, was expressed in the title or whether the said Zedekiah McDaniel and Francis M. Ewing, or either of them, hold commissions in the Confederate States Navy."[14]

With this resolution in hand, Freeman, with a second attorney, George Dixon, once again wrote Davis about getting on with the settlement of the claim. On April 5, Freeman wrote: "Several weeks since the undersigned had the honor to present to the President the petition of Messrs. McDaniel and Ewing, accompanied by a joint resolution of Congress directing the adjustment of their claim for the destruction of the enemy's gunboat Cairo. Having received no intimations of the President's views in the [illegible] they beg to be informed if any thing remains to be done on the part of claimants to enable them to have the benefit of said act of Congress."[15]

In accordance with the requirement of the act, a board of naval officers needed to be formed to determine the value of the *Cairo*. On May 21, Secretary of the Treasury C. G. Memminger wrote to Davis asking for guidance in handling the joint resolution he had received from Congress ordering him to pay McDaniel and Ewing.[16] On May 15, Mallory had appointed a board of naval officers to establish a value for the *Cairo*. The officers of that board, meeting at Richmond, were Captain S. S. Lee, Commander R. G. Robb, and Chief Naval Constructor J. L. Porter. On May 20, they returned their findings based on the statements of Sydney Hugh McAddam and Charles Brooke:

Hull complete 512 tons	C $130	$66,560.00
Anchors, cables, casks		2,360.00
Iron armor 2-1/2	250 tons "a 8	44,800.00
Engines and boilers complete		19,120.00
Protection to boilers, wood and iron		4,375.25

Provisions and paymasters stores	3,575.00
Master's store	1,750.50
Three (3) 42 pdr rifled and carriages	2,540.20
Four (4) 8 in. shell guns @ 3 cwt.	2,797.92
Four (4) 32 pdr. 57 cwt.	2,032.14
Two (2) 12 pdr boat howitzers	725.00
Fifty (50) muskets	500.00
Fifty (50) cutlasses	200.00
Two (2) 20 pdr. Parrots (omitted above)	1,016.08
Fifty (50) boarders pistols	250.00
Gun tackles and breechings: 13 guns	150.00
Fifty (50) pounds shell and fifty (50) do shot	3,395.50
10,000 lbs powder	2,120.00
	$158,767.61[17]

Memminger, who included copies of all these documents in his letter to Davis and did not want to be caught in the middle of a fight between Congress and the president, wrote Davis, "I have concluded to submit the whole matter at this stage to Congress for its further instructions."[18]

Upon receipt of the material from Congress, Davis wrote a lengthy letter to the Congress on June 11, 1864, explaining his veto of its action and refusal to pay the claim. After outlining the history of the claim, Davis got to the core of his problem:

> My objections to the present joint resolution are:
>
> 1st. That there is error of fact in its recital that a board of naval officers had reported that the "Cairo" was destroyed "by means of a torpedo invented and used by the memorialists." Not only is it a mistake that such a report was made, but it is believed to be very questionable whether the torpedo was an original invention of the memorialists.
>
> 2d. The claimants failed to give the Government the consideration which the law requires as a condition of the right to reward—namely, such a description of the alleged invention as would enable the Government to enjoy freely its reserved rights of using the invention in its own service.
>
> 3d. The most serious objection is this, that the service on which the claim is founded was rendered by officers of the Navy specially appointed and paid for this service. They did not make known to the Department when they were appointed that they proposed to use a special torpedo of their own invention, for the use of which they expected a reward. So far as is known to the Government, all the means, the materials, the expenditures of the torpedo service in the Yazoo River, including the pay and allowances of these claimants, were at the charge of the Government, and the service was performed under the control of a Navy officer of superior rank; nor was the sanction of any officer of the Government asked or given that these claim-

> ants should conduct torpedo experiments at public expense, without risk of time, labor, or capital of their own, and with the right to large reward in the event of success.
>
> No public officer charged with a special duty for which he is paid, and the means of performing which are also paid for by the Government, can be allowed to claim a reward for the performance of his duty without evils of the greatest character to the public service.
>
> Large numbers of Army and Navy officers have been employed in torpedo service and submarine defenses. Scarcely one has failed to suggest and essay new devices and combinations, many of which have proven successful. Numerous vessels have been destroyed, but the claim under consideration is the only one that has been presented to the attention of the government. None of the other officers seem to have imagined that it was not their duty to devote all their mind, talent, and inventive faculties in performing the service to which they were assigned without any pecuniary reward than the pay and allowances accorded by law to other officers of the same grade.[19]

Having argued around the legal points raised by Mallory, Davis raised the issue that most concerned him: "If the present joint resolution should give sanction to the opposite view of the duty of an officer, it is easy to perceive how injuriously it will affect the service. It is less easy to estimate the amount of claims on the Treasury that would thus be sanctioned." He then challenged Congress's opinion in the joint resolution: "My examination of the legislation leads me to a view of the policy of Congress quite different from that which would be implied by the passage of this joint resolution. The . . . acts . . . seem to me clearly to indicate a desire to encourage private enterprise. . . . They do not seem to me to have contemplated offering the same reward to the officers and seamen of the Navy." Having thus explained to Congress what it meant, he closed his letter by once more stressing the specter of the drain on the treasury: "I have deemed this full explanation of the facts and law of the case due to Congress as justifying the refusal to sign what is apparently an unimportant bill for the relief of private claimants, but is in reality the sanction of a principle deemed unsound and pernicious, involving in its consequences injury to the public service and *heavy demands on the public Treasury*" (emphasis added).[20]

By early 1865, the Confederate congress passed H.R. 361, a bill to centralize the intelligence, sabotage, and subversion services of the Confederacy. One of the main parts of the bill stated that compensation for services would be in accordance with the secret act of April 21, 1862, the same act relied on by McDaniel and Ewing in their claim.[21]

While McDaniel was actively pursuing his claim in Richmond between summer 1863 and spring 1864, he did not cease his intelligence operations. During the summer of 1863, he was apparently in contact with Brigadier General Gabriel Raines and engaged in various torpedo service activities. On September 21, 1863, McDaniel received his patent, No. 209, from the Confederate Patent Office. On October 22, still in Richmond, he signed a receipt voucher in the amount of $100 for "expenses incurred in experiments with shells, etc under orders of Colonel Stinns."[22] On November 17, G. W. Carrus applied to Seddon to "engage in the submarine corps of Z. McDaniel."[23] On November 18, McDaniel applied to Seddon for a pass for L. B. Boynton, "an Indian boy who is desirous of acting in my service within the lines of the enemy or otherwise. He understands the use of torpedoes and will make a valuable opertant."[24] On November 21, Special Orders Number 277 from the Adjutant and Inspector General's Office ordered Sergeant A. J. Stevens, Company E, Fifth Regiment, Texas Volunteers, detailed for "special service, and will report to Captain Z. McDaniel, in this city."[25] We can surmise from these activities that McDaniel was actively recruiting new members for his unit under some, possibly unofficial, arrangement with the secretary of war. It is also probable that McDaniel was operating under the supervision of Raines.

There were two distinct bureaus in the Confederate government concerned with torpedoes. One was the navy's Submarine Battery Service under Hunter Davidson, and the other was the War Department's Torpedo Bureau under Gabriel Raines. Both bureaus were authorized by act of the Confederate Congress in October 1862. The differentiation seemed to be that Davidson's operations were primarily in navigable waterways using electrically detonated torpedoes and Raines's were primarily on land, with some riverine work, and depended primarily on mechanical fuse devices such as the artillery friction primer.[26]

On February 29, 1864, Seddon authorized McDaniel to "form a company of men, not to exceed fifty in number, for secret service work against the enemy, under the regulations prescribed by this Department for such organizations. When he shall have enlisted and mustered his company into service for the war he will receive a commission as captain in the Provisional Army of the Confederate States without pay."[27] McDaniel's company was organized for secret service operations that primarily involved sabotage and unconventional warfare using explosives. McDaniel was also to report to General Gabriel Raines. McDaniel was commissioned as an army captain because of his change from the Submarine Battery Service, under the Navy Department, to land operations, under the War Department. This technical change of rank did not prevent him from conducting riverine operations. The annotation to the order, "without pay," indicates that revenue for the operations would come from the act of Congress authorizing remuneration for destroying enemy material. This method of remuneration may account for why there was so much documentation of secret service operations that succeeded and virtually no detailed information on those that failed.

McDaniel and Ewing's claim was dead. The Confederate Congress had no desire to do battle with the president over a private claim. Sometime before March 23, 1864, Isaac Brown sent a message to Thomas Weldon advising Weldon of McDaniel and Ewing's claim. Brown told Weldon that the claim was going to be paid and that Brown had notified the Navy Department that Burton and Weldon were entitled to a portion of the payment.[28] By the time Brown had his information in February–March 1864, the joint congressional resolution on McDaniel and Ewing's' claim had been passed. Brown was well connected in the Navy Department and was on the East Coast at that time. He might have believed that the joint resolution would result in payment of the claim. Weldon then began collecting statements from torpedo crew members and others who would support his position that he, not McDaniel or Ewing, conceived the idea of using friction primers to detonate the torpedo.

On May 12, 1864, Weldon wrote Brown a letter in which he outlined what he thought was the true story concerning the discovery of the friction primer detonator theory used in the torpedo that sank the *Cairo*. After first disavowing any monetary interest at the time of the invention, Weldon says:

> As the matter however has been brought to the attention of the Government, and a remuneration for its success required by persons who do not deserve it, I have determined to present you with this statement of the facts in the case, in order that, if there is any honor or award to be rendered, it may induce the government to bestow it upon those justly entitled to it. As you are familiar with the parties, and probably with those facts, permit me to rely upon your assistance to have retained whatever portion Mr. Burton and myself are entitled to, in the event any payment being proposed.

Weldon explained his version of the facts to Brown:

> The apparatus used by Mr. McDaniel failed to be effective. Mr. Burton whom you sent to assist him, informed me of this failure at Snyder's Bluff,

> where I was engaged in obstructing the Yazoo River. He was on his way to report to you at Yazoo City and had abandoned all hopes of success. Believing myself that an efficient torpedo could be made, I requested Mr. Burton to accompany me to Vicksburg to procure, if possible, material for the purpose which was accomplished on the day following, at my own expense we returned to Snyder's Bluff the same night, and with some friction primers, which I obtained from Colonel Edward Higgins, and other materials brought from Vicksburg a torpedo was arranged; by two of which the "Cairo" was sunk. On the first trial the explosion was made by hand with but little effect; the next was by contact of the vessel and effective.

Brown replied by endorsement on the back of Weldon's letter:

> Respectfully returned for the use of Mr. Thos. Weldon whose statement regarding the part performed by himself and Mr. Burton in the destruction of the U.S.S. Cairo agrees with all the information official and otherwise that I had at the time of the affair taking place. In my official report of which I called the attention of the Navy Department to the valuable aid rendered by Mr. Weldon and Mr. Burton. Stating also that credit was due to Messrs. McDaniel and Ewing for having originated the attempts to destroy the enemys gunboats by torpedoes on the Yazoo River.[29]

A comparison of Brown's two letters brings out some interesting facts. In his first letter of December 1862, he supposes McDaniel and Ewing's success was due to a suggestion by Burton that friction primers be used.[30] Brown wrote: "Though full credit must be given Acting Masters McDaniel and Ewing for their success, I think that they were fortunate in obtaining Mr. Burton's aid as probably their immediate success was owing to a suggestion of *his* to use 'friction primers' instead of their method in setting off torpedoes." Yet in this endorsement to Weldon, he does not dispute Weldon's statement that Weldon came up with the idea. Brown's indecisive words in both documents indicate that he did not know whose idea it was to use friction primers. Many years later, Brown wrote, "I borrowed a five-gallon glass demijohn, and procuring from the army the powder to fill it and an artillery friction tube to explode it, I set these two enterprising men [McDaniel and Ewing] to work."[31]

In both letters he noted that McDaniel and Ewing initiated the torpedo operations in the Yazoo. Weldon obviously had no torpedoes farther up the Yazoo at his obstruction raft at Snyder's Bluff at the time McDaniel and Ewing were operating four miles downriver from him. Even Colonel Higgins, in an early December 1862 letter to Weldon, noted a separation between Weldon and the "torpedo people": "As Anthony's Ferry is in possession of the enemy I want you to hurry all you can in getting the [lighter] ready which you were directed to build for the government—Send it to me as soon as you can. The torpedo people seem to have knocked off work. They are perfectly idle—a few torpedoes now would be of great service." It is obvious from this letter that the only torpedo operations and the only "torpedo people" were McDaniel and Ewing's crew. Of even more importance, this letter probably focused Weldon's thoughts when he was confronted by the disappointed Burton, headed back to Yazoo City to report to Brown. If Weldon had torpedoes in operation at that time, it was logical for him to test the friction primers there instead of sending Burton and Blake to McDaniel's location and taking supplies there. Certainly after the success of December 11 and 12, torpedoes were placed in the river below Weldon's raft. On December 25, 1862, Higgins wrote Weldon that General Stephen D. Lee had advised him of the arrival of the Union transports and the expected imminent attack (Sherman's December 1862 Chickasaw Bayou expedition). He closed by urging Weldon to "chime in all you can with your torpedo arrangements. Try and get those down tonight."[32] At least by December torpedoes were being considered for use at the obstruction raft.

Weldon sought, and received, statements from John Beggs, Edward Blake, Colonel Edward Higgins, Francis M. Tucker, David Curry, James J. Dees, and John Stancil.

Beggs was in Demopolis, Alabama, in March 1864, when he wrote to Weldon. Weldon was in Demopolis on May 12, 1864, when he wrote to Brown. Beggs does not say whose idea it was to use friction primers. He only notes Burton's arrival at McDaniel's torpedo camp, departure, and return two days later. He does attribute a statement to Burton that Weldon had obtained some friction primers from Higgins, saying that "with the materials referred to, the torpedoes were made, by which the Cairo was sunk."[33]

Blake, who worked for Weldon on the obstruction raft at Snyder's Mills, wrote on March 26, 1864: "You [Weldon] then expressed your belief that it was practicable to make a torpedo by which the enemy could be injured stating at the same time that you were going to Vicksburg to procure materials for the purpose and requested Burton to go with you which he did. You returned with the materials the night following and got some friction primers from Col. Higgins and on the next day you directed me to make some necessary appliances and go with Burton for the purpose of trying your torpedo."[34]

Tucker, who was illiterate, tendered a statement very similar to Blake's: "Burton [returned to report to] Capt. Brown. After two days absence he returned bringing with him various materials which he stated you had purchased at Vicksburg for the purpose of trying a torpedo on a plan of your own. He also brought some friction primers, which he stated you had obtained from Col. Higgins. . . . A carpenter by the name of Bl[ake] [was] with Burton whom he stated you [sent] to assist in the operation. With the primers and materials [which] you sent, some torpedoes were [made] on your plan." Curry corroborated the previous statements: "Burton then left us as he stated to report the plan a failure. On the second day following, he returned in company with a carpenter whose name I think was Blake. They brought with them white lead, tallows, gutta percha, ropes, wire, friction primers, weights for anchors, pulleys and a lot of demijohns etc all of which Burton stated had been purchased by you at Vicksburg for the purpose of trying torpedoes upon a plan of your own which was immediately done."[35]

James Dees, then in Clinton, Louisiana, in a letter to Weldon the next day, July 5, reported similar observations to those of Curry: "[Burton] would report them [McDaniel's torpedoes] as a failure in about two days from the time he left he returned again in company with a carpenter I think his name was Blake they brought with them a quantity of materials of various kinds which Burton stated was purchased by you at Vicksburg with thies materials torpedoes were made upon a plan proposed by you and entirely different from those made by McDaniel his being ignited by means of a percussion cap and yours by means of a friction primer his powder being in a tin can with a pipe as described and yours being in a demijohn."[36] This is the only description of McDaniel's early Yazoo torpedoes as being made of tin cans and pipes. All of McDaniel's and Ewing's statements clearly describe the torpedoes as being wicker-covered glass demijohns. But McDaniel was known to use soldered metal containers.[37]

Armed with these statements, sometime late in 1864 Weldon wrote a short plea to the Confederate Congress: "Your petitioner begs leave to submit herewith accompanying papers showing that he caused the destruction to the property of the public enemy caused by blowing up of the U.S. Gunboat Cairo in the Yazoo River, State of Mississippi, on or about the 12th day of December A.D. 1862 and to solicit such reward for the service as your honorable body may think deserves by the service."[38] Apparently no one bothered to tell Weldon about Davis's scathing letter to the Congress in June, and no record can be found indicating that Weldon's claim was given any consideration. H. Clay Sharkey, in an article written about fifty years later, said, "Mr. Weldon claimed that the Confederate government had offered $50,000 for the first boat sunk by a mine or torpedo, but I learned that for some reason he never got his reward."[39]

On December 20, 1862, eight days after the *Cairo* went down, Lieutenant J. B. Poindexter, a former telegrapher and adjutant of the Third Mississippi Infantry Regiment, Sharkey's unit on Snyder's Bluff, wrote a letter to Mississippi Governor John Pettus:

> I take the liberty of addressing you to suggest the use of sub-marine batteries in the Mississippi. . . . The subject of sub-marine batteries I thoroughly understand and I think would be of great benefit to our nearly overrun state. My plan is to have demijohns filled with powder enclosed in air-tight boxes in order to make them float under the water but a very short distance which I can easily do by using gasses. And, then push them in the river with boats carried on wheels like boats for a pontoon bridge. Whenever a boat gets over them they are to be fired by electricity. The expense of fitting up these boats and cost of powder cannot exceed five thousand dollars including 100 batteries. *The plan of putting powder in glass was suggested to Capt. McDonald [sic] by me and it was very successful at this place.* [Emphasis added.][40]

If McDaniel ever knew about Weldon's claim, there is no record of it. His new opportunities in the field of secret service were blooming, and he did not need to think about the past.

5

There Has Been No Day When We Were Not Operating Somewhere

January 1864–June 1865

Some of McDaniel's secret service operations were recorded and became well known. Others, apparently, were not as well known or the records were destroyed. One operation that he might have conducted involved Bennett G. Burley and John A. Maxwell, both experienced saboteurs and commissioned as acting masters in the Confederate navy. Maxwell was described as "wiry" and "full six feet, with broad square shoulders, black hair, moustache and whiskers." Burley was a "stout, round-shouldered, deep full-chested man of two and twenty, with brown hair, blue eyes, quick with intelligence, and a fair beardless face." Burley, whose name is sometimes spelled "Burleigh," was the son of a master mechanic from Glasgow, Scotland, who had immigrated to New York.[1]

On March 30, 1864, Burley, Maxwell, and Daniel Lucas received a pass to Libby Prison in Richmond signed by General John Winder, the provost marshal, authorizing them to interrogate prisoners from Purnell's Legion who had been captured on the Eastern Shore of Virginia.[2] Burley and Maxwell had just returned from a successful operation on the Chesapeake Bay, where they assisted in the capture of Union troops, stores, and three vessels by a thirteen-man detachment of the Fifth Virginia Cavalry.[3] What they interrogated the Union prisoners about is not known, but on May 12, 1864, Burley, Maxwell, and a nine-man torpedo crew were surprised by a detachment of the Thirty-sixth U.S. Colored Infantry at Stingray Point. In the short skirmish, five of the Confederates were killed, and five, including Burley, were taken prisoner. Colonel Alonzo G. Draper, commanding the colored troops, reported that the torpedo crew consisted of "cavalry and marines, under command of . . . Burley and . . . Maxwell." Draper also reported that one man escaped, but that "Acting Master Maxwell and 4 others were killed." Colonel Draper was mistaken. The only escapee was Maxwell. Perhaps Burley told the Union troops that Maxwell was dead so as to give him an opportunity to escape. The prisoners were fortunate because "the colored troops would have killed all the prisoners had they not been restrained by Sergeant Price, who is also colored." Colonel Draper noted in his report that nine torpedoes were discovered and destroyed by his troops. Draper described the torpedoes as "constructed with tin cases, each containing about fifty pounds of powder."[4] Tin case torpedoes were used by both McDaniel and Raines.

Maxwell apparently was never captured, though Burley was captured a second time in September 1864 during John Yates Beall's abortive attempt to seize the *USS Philo Parsons* near Johnson's Island. Burley was detained in Canada for a while and then allowed to return to England in lieu of being turned over to United States authorities.

McDaniel had his detractors, and there was a great deal of rivalry among the torpedo groups. On May 21, 1864, Lieutenant Colonel J. A. Williams of the Confederate Engineers wrote to J. R. Fretwell: "Can you raise some men and bring down the 8 torpedoes via Drewry's Bluff? I can detail a few men here. I want them assigned for floating down upon the monitors that are shelling us. McDaniel has disappointed me."[5]

On February 11, 1865, W. S. Oldham, another entrepreneur seeking to break into the torpedo business, wrote to Jefferson Davis concerning his plans to sabotage Union targets by arson. He wrote: "First. The combustible material consists of several preparations and not one alone, and can be used without exposing the party using them to the least danger of detection whatsoever. The preparations are not in the hands of McDaniel, but are in the hands of Professor McCulloch, and known but to him and one other party, I understand."[6]

On June 20, 1864, McDaniel applied to Major William S. Barton, acting adjutant general, for passes and a four-mule team to transport three men to sabotage the Baltimore and Ohio Railroad. The requisition was approved by Raines, but the quartermaster general, A. R. Lawton, returned the request saying that "in the present confusion, I am unable to say positively that these are on hand in that portion of Virginia."[7] The request is annotated, "Declined—file." In 1860, the Baltimore and Ohio Railroad had tracks from Baltimore to Washington, D.C.; Baltimore to Martinsburg, West Virginia, to Cumberland, Maryland, to Grafton, West Virginia; from Grafton, to Parkersburg, West Virginia; and a separate track from Grafton to Wheeling. The proposed mission, if targeted against the western portion of the railway, would require significant travel over difficult terrain. The most likely portion of the railway to attack was the Baltimore-to-Martinsburg leg.

The three men designated for the mission against the Baltimore and Ohio were Captain James Gubbins, Company F, Fifth Louisiana Regiment, Lieutenant Samuel Harrison, Company D, Fifth Louisiana Regiment, and Oliver Kirtley, one of McDaniel's Kentucky-born operatives. McDaniel noted that these three men were "all selected with especial care and all experienced in operating within the enemy's lines."[8] Gubbins was an experienced twenty-seven-year-old combat officer who had been promoted through the ranks from private to captain. Originally from Jersey City, New Jersey, he worked before the war as a tinsmith, which would have given him skills critical to McDaniel's operations. Following his enlistment in the Confederate army at New Orleans in May 1861, he fought at Hanover Courthouse, Antietam, and Gettysburg, where he received his promotion to captain. He was wounded twice, captured four times, and escaped four times. His last escape was from Fort McHenry, Maryland, on May 15, 1864, just a month before McDaniel's request. He was killed in action at Cedar Creek on October 19, 1864.[9] Harrison was a twenty-four-year-old former clerk and had enlisted at New Orleans in May 1861. He was wounded at Winchester, Virginia, on September 19, 1864, and left in the enemy's hands with a minié ball wound to his left hip. He finished the war as a prisoner in a hospital.[10] Between May and August 1864, both Gubbins and Harrison are shown only as "present for duty" on their muster roll so it is possible they made a foray against the enemy during that time. Oliver Kirtley remained on McDaniel's staff for future missions.

Some idea of the scope of McDaniel's operation is revealed in a voucher signed by McDaniel on January 20, 1864, paying him $3,307.82 for "labor fitting 3,953 wooden fuze plugs to 53,352 lbs condemned shells. . . . 3,233-24 pdrs; 381 'Parrotts' 15-1/2 pdrs; 141-8 in mortars."[11] The application is annotated, "sub-terra shell for DfC [defense]." These "land torpedoes," several examples of which were found late in the twentieth century, were ordinary artillery shells fused using a Gabriel Raines invention that consisted of a threaded plug and bushing which contained an explosive mixture through its length into the main charge. The explosive mixture was ignited when an unsuspecting soldier stepped on the firing cap above the mixture causing the cap to ignite the mixture and explode the main charge. The firing cap contained potassium chlorate (50 percent), antimony sulfide (30 percent), and ground glass (20 percent) and was very sensitive to pressure. McDaniel noted that his unit supported the defense of Richmond in the summer of 1864: "We did all in our power to aid in the defense of Richmond, wherever permitted to operate—with sub-terra shell arranged and connected in batteries along the roads & with torpedoes in the James [River]—were constantly under the orders of Gen. Ransom, then commanding—; one whole available force in the city being at his disposal and frequently in his employment."[12]

Probably McDaniel's most significant operation, other than the *Cairo*, was initiated in July 1864. Sometime before July 26, 1864, McDaniel had given John A. Maxwell a mission order and some equipment. Maxwell was to remain behind the enemy's lines for as long as possible and do as much damage as possible. The important piece of equipment he was given was a "horological torpedo," known today as a time bomb. The bomb consisted of twelve pounds of powder in a box, a clockwork device, and a friction primer attached to the clock.[13] Maxwell left Richmond on July 26, 1864, accompanied by R. K. Dillard, who "was well acquainted with the localities." It took the pair eight days to travel from Richmond to Isle of Wight County, just west of Portsmouth. There, according to Maxwell, they discovered that "immense supplies of stores" were being landed at City Point, a major Union supply depot located at the confluence of the Appomattox and James rivers. It was also General Grant's headquarters. Maxwell and Dillard decided to place the time bomb on one of the ships and blow it up. It took them another seven days to travel from Isle of Wight County back to City Point, all the while in Union-controlled territory. Maxwell noted that they traveled mostly at night and "crawled upon our knees to pass the east picket line."[14]

Maxwell and Dillard arrived at City Point before daybreak on August 9. Maxwell, the more experienced saboteur, left Dillard behind, entered the Union supply facility; and cautiously made his way to the wharf area. He observed the captain of a barge leave the barge and proceed out of the area. Maxwell told a sentry who challenged him that he had orders from the captain to place his box containing the time bomb aboard the barge. Maxwell hailed a worker on the barge and, setting the timer, gave the box to the worker with orders to take it aboard.

Maxwell did not know that he was on the magazine wharf, that the barge was laden with high explosives, and that it was the only vessel in the port filled with explosives. The barge contained seven hundred boxes of artillery ammunition, two thousand boxes of small arms ammunition, six to seven hundred blank cartridges, and one keg of mortar powder. At 11:30 A.M., Maxwell and Dillard, who moved a small distance away but could see the wharf area, observed the largest explosion they had ever seen. Dillard was deafened and Maxwell "severely shocked," but both escaped "without lasting injury."

At City Point, a quiet Tuesday morning was suddenly the scene of deadly bedlam. When the smoke had cleared, 43 men were dead and 126 wounded. Two million dollars worth of military stores, equipment, and vessels went up in smoke. Colonel Theodore B. Gates, post commandant, wrote immediately to Captain Thomas Schuyler, the acting assistant adjutant general: "It is impossible to account for the occurrence. The men on the boat 'Kendrick' were all killed and no one else can give any explanation. Timber, exploding shell, small arms ammunition and solid shot filled the air and showered down on every hand, extending beyond my quarters. The ordnance boat 'Kendrick' and a barge 'The General Meade' were blown to fragments. The warehouse just completed was destroyed and much government property ruined."[15] Most of the killed and wounded were enlisted personnel and black laborers assigned to the magazine wharf area. Reports indicated that Private August Tessing (or Thessing) was probably the guard with whom Maxwell spoke. Tessing, who had exclusive charge of the ammunition handling personnel, was a German immigrant in the Union army and allegedly spoke poor English, which may help to account for Maxwell's success. Tessing was blown to bits in the explosion.

Maxwell and Dillard beat a hasty retreat and continued their assigned mission against enemy forces. Leaving City Point, they proceeded to the

Warwick River, where, with Acting Master W. H. Hinds, CSN, and a small group, they captured the *Jane Duffield*, bonded the ship, paroled the captain, and took one of the crew hostage to ensure compliance with the parole. They continued to operate on the James River at night but had no further successes. At Smithfield, they were discovered and decided to suspend operations because they were being pursued by Union troops.

While Maxwell and Dillard were on their operation, McDaniel continued to battle the military bureaucracy. On August 26, 1864, three of McDaniel's operatives were arrested in Mobile, Alabama. W. F. Bullock, Jr., assistant adjutant general to General Dabney H. Maury, wrote to Maury alleging that McDaniel was selling certificates of membership in his company to conscripts so they might avoid regular service. Bullock said that one such certificate was sold for $30,000 but provided no proof.[16]

Bullock's rantings convinced Maury to forward the matter to the War Department. Maury concurred that the "secret service" was an evil to be eliminated: "From the characters of the people whom I have observed engaging in this unmanly warfare, we have no guaranty that they will consider anything besides their individual interests under all circumstances, and it is probable that those of them who enter the lines of the enemy are his agents as well as our own."[17]

On September 17, 1864, Robert J. Breckinridge, who was commissioned by McDaniel to enlist company members, responded to Seddon's comment that he had received Bullock and Maury's letter. After a detailed recitation of his personal involvement in the formation and operations on behalf of McDaniel's company, Breckinridge wrestled with the age-old intelligence problem of how to satisfy bureaucracies without sacrificing the secrecy of operations: "The great difficulty in this service has been, that every Provost Marshal and Enrolling Officer, through whose office one of the certificates were passed has interested himself to discover the entire working of the organization and the *particular business* of the person holding the certificate. If this information was given then it would no longer be *secret service*."[18]

Also on September 17, McDaniel wrote to Seddon requesting that he order Maury to release the three men in Mobile and cease interfering with his men. McDaniel succinctly described the crux of the problem: "The organizations of the Secret Service Corps under the Act of Congress, are not understood beyond the War Depart. & the Superintending General.

Nor can we enter into explanations to those who are prejudiced against them. For want of knowledge, because the Service would cease to be *Secret* & *special*; but we confidently hope by earnest exertion to vindicate by results the wisdom of Congress & yourself in employing these organizations."[19]

While Breckinridge and McDaniel were writing to Seddon, he was writing to McDaniel asking for an explanation and assurances based on what Maury reported to him: "Reports have reached this Department that you are exceeding the privilege of recruiting a company for secret service allowed you and that of your men ostensibly engaging transportation for such service are abusing it for purposes of speculation. You are ordered and directed to forward at once a roll of the men of your company with a statement showing their residences and how employed, and likewise whether any are engaged to your knowledge in trade and speculation."[20]

As a result of Seddon's order, McDaniel wrote a lengthy letter on September 20, 1864, fully describing the formation, operations, and membership of his organization. But for the needs of the bureaucracy, we would not have any information on Captain McDaniel's Company, Secret Service.

> In conformity with your direction of the 17th inst. I have the honor to enclose herewith a roll of the men of my company, accompanied by the statement therein required. From an inspection of this paper it will be perceived that the reports that I had "exceeded the privilege of recruiting the company allowed" me are wholly unfounded. Twenty-seven men are all who, to this time, have been recruited and constitute all who bear certificates of membership. Colo. R. J. Breckenridge has informed me that he had addressed you a letter in reply to certain reports which had reached you from Mobile in which he detailed at some length the operations of the company since its organization to the present. To the report which has reached you also that my men ostensibly engaged in Secret Service & enjoying transportation for the same, are abusing it for the purpose of trade and speculation, I reply that I have no knowledge or information direct or indirect of the practice of any such abuses by my men nor that any of them are engaged in trade & speculation. Nor can I report it that any of them have rendered themselves thus obnoxious; but if the names of the persons charged be furnished me with a responsible accusation, their conduct shall be inquired into, and if the accusation is sustained, they shall be promptly turned over to the enrolling officers for other duty. I have no use for such men. As for transportation, I have never taken it from the government nor authorized its employment for persons or freight unless their destination

was in good faith in an enterprise against the enemy; and the truth is, my men have more frequently paid for their transportation than drawn it. In the services which my company performed during the administrations on Richmond last summer, on the land & along the James, transportation was obtained at the company's expense, and in several cases where unfortunately captured had to be paid for by the company. It has also lost two valuable animals and other means of transportation in like service.

Upon the issuing of your authority to me in February last (29 Feb) Colo. Breckenridge set about the proper organization of the company on the basis understood at the time of the letter of authority & set out in the application filed by him for it—the details of which he has already communicated to you. He is still engaged in the same service.

We commenced operations with but seven men and since then there has been no day when we were not operating somewhere, to carry out the design of the company and to justify the confidence of the department.

We did all in our power to aid in the defense of Richmond, wherever permitted to operate—with sub-terra shell arranged and connected in batteries along the roads & with torpedoes in the James—were constantly under the orders of Gen. Ransom, then commanding—; one whole available force in the city being at his disposal and frequently in his employment. So will they always be in like emergencies. There is no member of my command who is not fully impressed that he is regularly mustered into the service for special and secret duty and that when not so engaged, when the necessity occurs, he must join in the general defense. Nor do I believe I have a man who would in such a case *attempt* to skulk behind his certificate as a refuge from the common peril. It is true charges have been preferred against two of my men *McCorkle* & *Parrish* from Lynchburg; but their cases are now pending before the conscript bureau and I understand they will be able fully to acquit themselves as I believe they will be. It is an impression to the contrary of this which has obtained among some (officials among them) which has caused us a great deal of trouble and excited their heated prejudices against Secret Service.

They look upon its contribution as an evil which they in their spheres must regulate & restrain. Because they cannot see all and have all explained to them, they conclude something must be wrong, because they cannot know all. But their objections & prejudices when resolved go entirely to the impolicy of such organizations at all, & therefore they seek to thwart them, ignorant that they were authorized by Congress & established by its sanction. Whilst the Service is liable to abuses it is in like proportion liable to unjust suspicion.

I have now as the list exhibits a number of men employed (members of the company) at our outposts and within the enemy's lines—especially in Shermans rear and along the Mississippi River who are aiming at the enemy.

From time to time we have employed as necessity required the services of non-conscripts, exempts to whose services have been paid for. They were in no sense members of the company nor protected by its certificate.

Those members now in Richmond or near, have nearly all been actively engaged in the Service & are ready for it again when other enterprises are ready which are now in contemplation. The expenses of maintaining these operatives thus, transportation within and without the enemies lines at the various points of operation—the preparation of torpedoes and other materials are all defrayed out of the means of the company.

Whilst I am out of communication with my men at distant points I have good reason to believe that some of the property losses which the enemy has recently severely suffered at New Orleans, Louisville, St. Louis, Cairo, by loss of boats on their rivers and at other points has been caused by a portion of my men who were sent for exactly such work & who are yet in the enemys lines.

From the fact that the enemys papers have heralded no "*revelations*" of our plans I conclude that all men have proven true and are silently and effectively at their work of impairing the property strength of the enemy. They were secretly furnished with the means & facilities for their purposes. Upon notification that Brig. Gen. Raines had been stationed in this city, I according to orders, reported to him and handed in a roll of my company, have since submitted my operations to his judgment & been most materially assisted by his superintendence and instruction.

Nothing has been withheld from him of the character of my company. The means it employs or the ends it seeks to obtain.

I am aware that this Service is liable to abuse, but such, Sir, has been the generous support which you have given my enterprise whenever appealed to, that I have felt under increased obligation to keep it as far as I could free from such aspersions as the reports to you have as I know, unjustly cast upon it. Such assistance as our company has been able to extend has been freely afforded to others engaged in similar Service.

If the statements made to you have taken the shape of impuning to me a guilty knowledge of these alleged abuses—or a fraudulent enlistment in excess of my authority, I have most respectfully to beg that I may be speedily furnished with the charges distinctly made, & that I may be confronted with my accusers & his witnesses, for an investigation in such made as may not derogate from the Service & as yourself may designate.[21]

Accompanying McDaniel's letter was a listing of his company's members and their disposition:

Z. McDaniel	Captain	Commanding
Joseph C. Frank[22]	1st Lieut.	Behind enemy lines Ky
J. N. Amiss[23]		Behind enemy lines Mo

William H. Berry[24]	Behind enemy lines Va (R)[25]
C. M. Bosker[26]	Awaiting orders Va (R)
E. W. Breeden[27]	Awaiting orders Va (R)
J. Bunch[28]	Awaiting orders Augusta Ga
G. H. Burnett[29]	Behind enemy lines Ky
Stephen Burns[30]	Awaiting orders Augusta Ga
J. R. F. Burroughs[31]	Awaiting orders Va (R)
S. M. Corkle[32]	Awaiting outcome of conscript bureau action Lynchburg
J. G. Dill[33]	Awaiting orders Va (R)
D. J. Dillahunt[34]	Under orders & detained in Mobile by General Maury's orders
W. S. Dupree[35]	Awaiting orders Va (R)
W. H. Gwice[36]	Awaiting orders in Richmond (Vicksburg, Ms)
B. M. Harris[37]	Awaiting orders Va (R)
R. D. James[38]	Sick in Richmond Va (R)
James Keelon[39]	Behind enemy lines Va (R)
J. K. Keen[40]	Awaiting orders, Pittsylvania County, Va
Oliver Kurtley[41]	Behind enemy lines Ky
Charles Loneman[42]	Awaiting orders Va (R)
William Leonard[43]	Mobile, Ala, detention with two others
F. P. McCarty[44]	Behind enemy lines
G. W. Neville[45]	Under orders and in charge of material to different points, Ky.
W. H. Parrish[46]	Awaiting outcome of conscript bureau action Lynchburg
R. W. Scott[47]	Behind enemy lines Tenn
Elias E. Sinclair[48]	In charge of company business Richmond Va (R)
S. M. Williams[49]	Mobile, Ala, detention.

Recapitulation:

2— Officers (1 behind enemy lines)

26— Enlisted

1—Company clerk

1—Sick

3—Detention in Mobile, Ala

2—Awaiting conscript bureau action
1—On orders delivering materials
7—Behind enemy lines
11—Awaiting orders (2 in Augusta, Ga; 1 in Pittsylvania County, Va; 8 in Richmond[50]

The backgrounds of some of these men indicate that they were known to McDaniel before the war. Some were from Barren County, Kentucky; one was his brother-in-law. Such arrangements were not unusual during the Civil War. According to William Tidwell, "One of the results of the loose organization of [Confederate] intelligence was that it made the personal relationships among the individuals in the components very important. The need for fast results combined with the lack of such modern devices as the polygraph and a trained investigation organization made it necessary for the managers to recruit help from among people they already knew they could trust. That meant that relatives, friends, and neighbors of the [heads of intelligence units] might very likely turn up in some intelligence-related activity."[51]

It must have taken several months to straighten out the matter concerning McDaniel's company. On October 28, 1864, the Adjutant and Inspector General's Office issued Special Orders 257, paragraph XXV, ordering Major General J. L. Kemper to assign an assistant adjutant and inspector general to inspect McDaniel's company and "ascertain if their authority has been observed in the recruitment of men and their employment." A report was to be made to Kemper and forwarded to the War Department.[52]

On December 2, 1864, McDaniel wrote again to Seddon concerning the three men held prisoner in Mobile.

> I have the honor to request that three men of my command . . . Dillahunt . . . Leonard, and . . . Williams, detained by . . . Maury in Mobile and now on duty there under his orders be released and ordered to report to George B. Thompson of my command at Mobile who will shortly depart there upon an expedition against the shipping of the enemy.
>
> Mr. Thompson is a superior chemist and mechanic, and has served faithfully with me since the organization of my company. He put up the calcium lights for . . . Maury in Mobile Bay and is now engaged in processing electrical batteries for the defense of the same place.[52]

McDaniel's letter was accompanied by endorsements from General Raines vouching for Thompson and from Seddon to the adjutant general ordering the release of the three men so they could report to Thompson as his assistants.

Maxwell and Dillard arrived in Richmond on December 14, 142 days after they departed on their mission. On December 16, 1864, an event occurred that would alter McDaniel's life forever. He received the following communication from John Maxwell: "I have the honor to report that in obedience to your order, and with the means and equipment furnished me by you, I left this city 26th of July last, for the line of the James River, to operate with the Horological torpedo against the enemy's vessels navigating that river." Maxwell and Dillard returned from their foray in eastern Virginia and wrote a lengthy report concerning their actions, including the surprise explosion at City Point on August 9. McDaniel forwarded the report to General Raines with a simple endorsement, "Respectfully forwarded to Brigadier-General Raines. Z. McDaniel, Captain, Company A, Secret Service."[54] This is the only recorded mention of the designation Company A. It may have been a creation of McDaniel's to distinguish his company as the first of its kind because there was no apparent logical lettering of secret service companies formed by order of Secretary of War Seddon.

Nothing is known about McDaniel's company or its operations for the next three months. On March 27, 1865, Brigadier General Henry Gray, McDaniel's commander in the Bayou Teche operations in 1863, wrote to General John C. Breckinridge, then Confederate secretary of war, requesting that McDaniel and his company be transferred to his command on the Mississippi: "I confidently believe that with his aid I can blow up the stationary gun boats on the Mississippi from the mouth of the Red River to Lake Providence. It is likewise important to block adv in this way the Red River below Genl Buckner's defenses."[55]

Breckinridge forwarded the request to General Raines for comment, indicating that he would look favorably upon the transfer if Raines acceded. Raines begrudgingly agreed: "Capt. McDaniel's services are of much importance to my operations in checking the enemy's advance at Lynchburg, Va, with sub-terra shells. Yet believing that he can be more useful on the Mississippi as his transfer thereto I approve with each of his company as are under his immediate command. The Capt. before he leaves however should turn over his duties in Lynchburg to competent hands."[56] On March 28, 1865, Special Orders 73 commanded McDaniel to report to Gray as soon as he found someone to replace him in Lynchburg.[57]

There was little McDaniel could do to help the Confederacy after this date. Richmond was occupied on April 3 by Union troops. Six days later, on April 9, General Robert E. Lee surrendered his forces at Appomattox, ending the war in Virginia. By the end of another week, John Wilkes Booth had killed Abraham Lincoln and the search for a great conspiracy began. Union conspiracy hunters pored over page after page of official Confederate letters and orders seized during the occupation of Richmond, seeking the clue that would tie the known Lincoln conspirators to the Confederate secret services.[58]

Although they never made such a connection, they did find many records that explained secret service actions during the war. One of those documents was Maxwell's report to McDaniel on the City Point explosion with McDaniel's endorsement to Raines.[59] In September 1865, General Rufus Ingalls wrote to General Montgomery C. Meigs that "it was assumed at the time that the explosion was the result of the carelessness on the part of someone in or near the barge, but the developments made in the trial of the assassins of the late President would show that it was the dastardly work of that infernal rebel torpedo bureau in Richmond."[60] Maxwell's report to McDaniel was entered into evidence at the trial of the Lincoln conspirators on June 20, 1865, by the Union prosecutors. But on June 3, two weeks earlier, perhaps for political reasons, General Henry W. Halleck wrote the following letter to Secretary of War Edwin M. Stanton: "I have just received the original official report of John Maxwell, of the rebel secret service, of the blowing up of the ordnance stores at City Point last year. It appears from this report that the explosion was caused by a horological torpedo placed on the barge by John Maxwell and R. K. Dillard, acting under the direction of Brig. Gen. G. J. Rains and Capt. Z. McDaniel. I have ordered the arrest of these persons, if they can be found, and will send you a copy of the report and endorsement."[61]

Zere McDaniel, the man whose charmed life allowed him to escape just ahead of Union forces in Kentucky, Memphis, Vicksburg, Fort Bisland, Alexandria, Port Hudson, Tullahoma, and Lynchburg, might not wait around for certain retribution.

Conclusion

Z. McDaniel Was Active in the Destruction of United States Property

July 1865–1870

Nothing is known about McDaniel's movements between March 1865 and sometime in 1867. Reconstruction of the South was proceeding. In McDaniel's native Pittsylvania County, Virginia, a man named Tucker from Maine was appointed commonwealth attorney. Tucker is said to have attempted to incite the freedmen against the local white population. Judge Gilmer, a staunch Virginian, spoke against Tucker publicly in front of the county courthouse. The Reverend Chiswell Dabney described the action:

> Tucker tried to resent Judge Gilmer's accusations but a very large man who was standing near named Zery McDaniel ascended the box Judge Gilmer had just vacated and expressed himself against Tucker in the strongest terms. He said: "I have lived in many parts of the earth, under 52 different governments and I have beheld every kind and variety of criminal; I have looked into the face of murder, arson and every crime known in the catalogue of sin, but"—and pointing his finger at Tucker—"that man standing there embraces in his features every characteristic of every crime known to man. None have I ever seen depicts so low a type of criminal as that cowardly scoundrel."[1]

McDaniel's actions were certain to bring him to the attention of the government and not endear him to the occupying Federal forces. He apparently did not know, or perhaps did not care, that a warrant had been issued for his arrest.[2]

I learned the remainder of the story of Zere McDaniel from family oral history. Sometime after the courthouse incident, McDaniel was at home with his wife and children. A runner came to the house and warned McDaniel that Union troops were on the way to arrest him. Gathering what items they could carry, Zere and Elizabeth put the children in a wagon and took off. Cresting a nearby mountain, they looked back to see their home being put to the torch by Union soldiers. Fearing retribution, they fled south to family members then living in northeastern Georgia, near Appling. When they told of their narrow escape they were hidden in the nearby swamps.

In about 1870, Zere McDaniel caught a fever and died. Fearing that Union forces might learn of his family's whereabouts, his Georgia family buried him in an unmarked, or wrongly marked, grave, the site of which is unknown. Elizabeth left their son, little Zere, with the family in Georgia.[4] Taking Quinlinnia, she returned to her family in Allen County, Kentucky,[5] where she died in about 1876.

Little Zere later married Louise "Lulu" Hardin and had five children.[6] They all remained in the northeast Georgia area, where Zere worked as a timber cruiser. One night he killed a man in a fight and was forced to flee Georgia. He returned years later to Lulu, bringing gold he had mined in California. The gold was made into a ring for her.

Quinlinnia remained with her mother in Kentucky. On May 9, 1880, at the Monroe County home of Rufus Hibbit, a local blacksmith, she was married by A. W. Potter to Albert Sidney Weir, a dentist.[7] Hibbit's wife, Kate, stood nearby holding the Hibbits' six-month-old son, Zera.[8]

Among the papers in Z. McDaniel's compiled military record in the National Archives is a typescript document, written on official United States government stationery. The letter has no addressee, and it is not signed.

WAR DEPARTMENT

THE ADJUTANT GENERAL'S OFFICE

WASHINGTON

In reply refer to ORD May 21, 1934

There are on file a number of papers indicating that Z. (also borne as Zedekiah) McDaniel of Kentucky was active in the destruction of United States property by means of torpedoes in 1862 and 1863.

On February 29, 1864, he was authorized to enlist a company of men for secret service against the enemy.

On September 20, 1864, he signed as Captain a list of recruits of his company and by order dated March 28, 1865, he was directed to report to Brigadier General Henry Gray, commanding on the Mississippi River.

His arrest was ordered by General Halleck June 3, 1865[9]

The outcome of the battle of Vicksburg was rarely in doubt. Overwhelming Union siege forces starved the Confederate bastion and civilians into submission, although it was not as easy as they thought it would be. The sinking of the *Cairo* put Union commanders on notice that the Confederates were not going to quit without a fight and the Union advantage in naval forces would be partially offset by Confederate defenses. Sherman's humiliation at Chickasaw Bayou confirmed that fact. Subsequent forays into the Yazoo were slowed significantly following the sinking of the *Cairo*. The necessity of clearing torpedoes resulted in the Union naval delay and loss on December 24, 1862, at Snyder's Bluff and the later actions near Yazoo City where the Eads ironclad USS *DeKalb* was sunk by one of Isaac Brown and Francis Shepperd's torpedoes.

In the overall scheme of the Civil War, the sinking of the *Cairo* was important for several reasons. It was the first recorded sinking of a man-of-war in combat by torpedoes. The use of torpedoes, later called naval mines or sea mines, would revolutionize naval defense, forcing combat vessels to proceed with caution, slowing their advance, channelizing them, and making them better targets for shore-based gunners. Torpedoes brought naval warfare to a new era, often frustrating commanders. At Mobile Bay in 1864, the monitor USS *Tecumseh* hit a Confederate torpedo and sank instantly with the loss of most of her crew. The next ship in line, the *Brooklyn*, began backing to avoid the torpedo line, threatening to create total havoc in the Union battle line. Admiral Farragut, aboard his flagship, the *Hartford*, perhaps believing in his own invincibility or Providence, ordered the *Hartford* forward and his helmsman to disregard the danger of torpedoes. "Damn the torpedoes, full speed ahead!" Had he struck one, his attitude might have changed. Ultimately, more Union naval vessels were sunk or destroyed during the Civil War by torpedoes than any other combat action or method.

The sinking of the *Cairo* was the result of a chain of events. If McDaniel and Ewing had not made the lonely, valiant efforts they did for many months in attempting to construct torpedoes on the Yazoo, Burton would never have been sent to assist them. If Burton had not been sent, he would not have had the opportunity to discuss torpedoes with Weldon. If Weldon had not been pushed by a letter from Higgins and provided the materials, Burton might not have been able to bring them. If Burton had not returned, the torpedoes would not have been built in time and the *Cairo* would not have been sunk on December 12, 1862. We do not know for sure whose idea it was to use friction primers. It does not matter now. In their futile efforts to gain fortune and fame, Weldon, McDaniel, and Ewing created an archive of information about what occurred in the days surrounding December 12, 1862. This archive made it possible to tell the story of the USS *Cairo*. The Confederate story is now told.

Appendix

Confederate Documents Relating to the Sinking of the USS *Cairo* on 12 December 1862

Following are copies of documents referred to in this book. The originals are in the National Archives and Records Administration, Washington, D.C., in Record Group 45, Vessel Papers, File C225, USS *Cairo*.

The McDaniel-Ewing Claim, March 23, 1863
Isaac N. Brown's Letter to Secretary of the Navy S. R. Mallory, December 25, 1862
Statement of D. M. Currie, February 10, 1863
Statement of George B. Stewart and Isaac G. Johnston, February 14, 1863
Statement of Charles T. Brooke, February 18, 1863
Statement of T. O. Davis, February 25, 1863
Statement of George Work, July 17, 1863
Zere McDaniel's Letter to Jefferson Davis, July 18, 1863
The Thomas Weldon Claim, Undated
Statement of John Beggs, March 23, 1864
Statement of Edward C. Blake, March 26, 1864

The McDaniel-Ewing Claim, March 23, 1863

Confederate States of America
Navy Department
To
Jefferson Davis
President

The undersigned citizens of the said Confederate States respectfully represent that since the 21st day of April, A.D. 1862 they have invented and constructed a new mashine and a new method of destroying the armed vessels of the enemys of said Confederate States. That between the 21st day of April 1862 and the 12th day of December 1862 they constructed and placed said mashinery in the lower Yazoo River about four miles below Snyder's Mill where the enemys gunboats were expected to appear. Said mashinery consisted of eighteen or twenty submarine batteries or torpedoes (a more particular description of which is on file in the Navy Department or will be filed therewith) Those batteries were constructed of five gallon glass demijohn filled with powder and connected by trigger wires with friction primers attached to and inserted in the powder through the closed necks of the demijohns—the torpedoes were anchored in the River at a distance about the width of a boat a part, they were sunk to a depth of five and a half feet below the surface of the River and so arranged and located that the enemys boats, in passing up the River at that point, must necessarily run upon some one or more of the trigger drawing the friction primers and firing a torpedo and each side of the boat thereby producing instantaneous explosion and destruction of the vessel.

On the 12th day of December last between ten and eleven o'clock of that day five of the enemys armed vessels appeared below the batteries shelling the River banks furiously. Four of their boats halted some seventy five yards below the torpedoes while they armed and Ironclad Gunboat Cairo came up slowly and cautiously advanced. Three persons stood near the bow of the boat—no other were in sight—a voice from the boat cried "How is it in the front?"—A voice from the pilot house cried "All clear"—At this moment the Cairo struck the trigger rod between two batteries, producing simultaneous explosion of the two and a consequent destruction and emersion of the vessel, which disappeared with all on board within two minutes from the moment of the explosion.

Affiant Ewing was standing on the River bank at a distance of forty to sixty yards in full view of the Cairo at the time of the explosion and witnessed the whole scene.

The Cairo struct the trigger of the batteries at an acute angle exploding one torpedo on her left side near her bow and another on her right side amidships—Portions of her timber were crushed and strewn on the water, the anchor and chain which hung on the left on the bow of the boat was thrown high above the vessel—she struggled a moment in the whirlpool created by the explosion—a cloud of white smoke arose above her, when she is instantly sunk. Only three of her crew were observed to float on the surface, but whether they survived and escaped affiant is not informed. The steamer below the Cairo threw out small boats—landing men on both sides of the river, when affiant—retired to a distance of about four hundred yards. The enemy continued to shell with all their batteries while their men in small boats apparently surveyed the water and river banks in the vicinity of the wreck and searched for and destroyed some of our remaining torpedoes. When the gun boats first approached we had only fourteen men in camp near the torpedo batteries, and they were unarmed—There was but one rifle in the party most of the encampment immediately retired beyond range of the gun boats—some four or five only remaining in the vicinity of affiant and under protection of the levee. The gun boats retired down the river about four o'clock as affiant believes. When affiant and several of the men returned to the scene of the wreck where we saw a large number of the fragments of the Cairo and her furniture. There was no current in this part of the river and portion of the wreck remained floating on the surface. We had not boat and could not go out to the Cairo that night. The next day we procured boats and sounded for and found the wreck—her deck was about eight feet below the surface of the water—by means of a pole and hook attached thereto we raised matresses, blankets and hammocks—a long anchor chain and many other articles.—We found several long pieces of gilded work, indicating an elegant and costly finish of the cabins. We also found a piece of the timber of the boat on which was marked "Flag Officer Foot, Cairo" which we supposed indicated the name of the vessel. We subsequently learned from the enemy that the vessel sunk was the Cairo—an iron clad gun boat registered in the US Navy Register, as affiant is informed, as being of 512 tons burthen and carrying thirteen guns. We also found the bouy ropes which held the torpedoes to their place. They were entangled in the wreck of the boat so that they could not be withdrawn. This ropes extented from the bank of the river to the torpedoes. Where they were found after the explosion, and indicated with certainty the location of the exploded batteries.—Your petitioners refer to the affidavits of A. Lacy, T. O. Davis, D. M. Currie, Chas. Brooke, Isaac S. Johnson and Geo. B. Stuart, herewith filed.—also to the telegrams and report of Commander Isaac N. Brown on file in the Navy Department, including the description of the torpedoes and the mashinery applied in the use of the same, which is a part of Commander Brown's report of December 20th 1862.

Your petitioners are unable to state the number of men on board or the value of said gun boat Cairo and her armament. They are advised that the President is authorized by law to appoint a Board of Naval Officers whose duty it will be to ascertain the number of the enemy destroyed, make the valuation of the vessel and her armament, and submit the same for the approval of the President (See Acts 2nd Sess., page 22, 26 Sec. 10 page 85, 86 & 1 Sess 1862 page 51). Your petitioners have applied to the Yankee Officers of the gunboat Indianola taken prisoners with that boat and now at Vicksburg, for the description and value of the Cairo. They were present with the Indianola in the Yazoo River when the Cairo was sunk. They admitted that they were well acquainted with Cairo and could give her description and value but declined to do so unless they were authoritatively called upon to testify. If the Board is not otherwise satisfied as to the value of the said Cairo and her armament, petitioners ask that the president of said board may direct an officer at Vicksburg to take the depositions of said officers of said Indianola at Vicksburg before they are exchanged, as that even may soon happen and their testimony thereby lost to petitioners.

Your petitioners further respectfully ask for speedy action on their petition as they and their families are destitute of the present means of subsistance. Petitioner McDaniel is fifty years of age, he has a wife and two children. At the beginning of the war he had a stock, farm and several negroes in Barren County, Kentucky, but the enemy has driven him from his home, stolen his slaves, stock and provisions, and deprived him of all his property and means of support for his familie.—Petitioner Ewing has a wife and three children dependant on his personal exertions for support—he has served as an independent Private with the Raymond Fancibles 12th Miss. Regiment for 15 months. he had previously lost his right arm—but fought with a breech loading Maynard rifle supported by a shoulder strap. He received for this service no pay. he is now compelled to provide for his familie. Having exhausted all his means while thus engaged in the service of the confederacy.

In behalf of their destitute families your petitioners therefore appeal to the President for immediate action on their petition.—with all the earnestness of men devoted alike to the cause of their country and the protection of those whom God has given them—While they cheerfully brave death themselves they cannot endure the anguish arising from the poverty of their wifes and children. They are anxious to remain in the Public Service, as they feel confident they can destroy the gun boats of the enemy with increased facility. They have invented a simple cheap and safe mode of approaching and destroying the enemys vessels unobserved by day or by night. Their man of war is simply a hollowed log with the natural interior—a cavity within of sufficient length and diameter to conceal one man at its bow and another at its stern.—A small hole for observations in front and rear and a rudder attached and submerged at the stern to enable a hand to direct its course upon the enemys vessel. The water fills the log to the level of the river but there remains a sufficient air chamber above the water in the log to sustaine life for several hours. Experiments have proven that a log-boat thus arranged will not turn over in the water, but maintain its position like other boats. The torpedo is submerged from five to six feet below another log acting as a float. A line is attached to the end of the float log and another to the friction primer inserted in the wreck [neck] of the torpedo. Those lines are wound upon a reel which is held by the men in the log-boat and the torpedo is thus drawn after them until it is brought in contact with the enemys vessel. The liens are then paid out from the reel until the log boat floats a safe distance from the torpedo when by sudden jerk of the line attached to the friction primer in the torpedo and explosion is produced and the enemys vessel is destroyed.

SEE NOTE BELOW.

We made preparations to fight the enemys gun boat Essex in daylight at Vicksburg when she was last there, but were prevented by orders to the contrary. We are now willing to fight the Essex or any other gunboat at Port Hudson or elsewhere.

With the aid of energetic and determined men these operations could be extented to the enemys fleets at Port Hudson, Vicksburg and Fort Pemberton—Also to the Cumberland and Tennessee Rivers or wherever the enemy appear upon a current that will float driftwood toward their vessels.

Your petitioners have already passed through the enemys fleet in this manner when below Vicksburg—touched one of their gunboats overheard conversation on board—then floated off with the current landed at a safe distance below and returned unharmed to the city—at night the performance is entirely safe and practicable and as a floating log attraks no attention in the day time, it might be ventured upon in the open light if demanded by the urgency of the occasion.

Petitioners therefore pray that the President will graciously consider the extreme hardship of their situation and order such immediate action on their claim as will enable them to return to relieve their families and continue to fight the enemy and destroy his men of war whenever they appear in our rivers—all of which is respectfully submitted.

Z. McDaniel
F. M. Ewing

NOTE: NB This method of using the torpedoes was not resorted to in the Yazoo River because the back water from the Mississippi River overpowered the downward current of the Yazoo River and produced still water which forced us to use stationary batteries and discharge them either from the shore by pulling a line attached to the friction primer or by the mode applied to the Cairo.

We have several other modes of using the torpedo which will be applied as occasion and situation may require.

F. M. Ewing

State of Virginia:

City of Richmond, to wit: This day personally appeared before me F.

M. Ewing whose name is signed to the forgoing writings and made oath to the truth of all the statements contained therein.

Given under my hand this 23rd of March, 1863.

J. L. Williams
Notary Public

Isaac N. Brown's Letter to Secretary of the Navy S. R. Mallory, 25 December, 1862

Yazoo City, Miss, Decbr. 25th, 1862

Hon. S. R. Mallory
Secy of Navy
Richmond, VA
Sir,

I had the honor recently to send to the Department, two telegrams regarding the torpido destroyed gunboat of the enemy in the lower Yazoo. No doubt now exists but that the destruction was complete and instantaneous involving perhaps the loss of every one on board—The boat seems to have been either the "Cairo" or "Cincinnati", both of which were iron clads of 13 guns. At the moment of its destruction, it was with four others ascending the Yazoo and shelling the banks to drive back our pickets—and intending no doubt to attack our defenses at Snyder's Mills from which they were still four miles distand. The four boats returned from the point of the explosion with it is reported the black flag flying. They have not since been seen in the Yazoo. I had before hearing of the success of Acting Masters McDaniel and Ewing send at the request of Maj. Gen. M. L. Smith, 1st Lt. F. E. Shepperd, to investigate the proceedings and some days before that time I had sent acting Gunner Burton, CSN, to the assistance of the torpedo party. Though full credit must be given Acting Masters McDaniel and Ewing for their success, I think that they were fortunate in obtaining Mr. Burtons aid as probably their immediate success was owing to a suggestion of his to use "friction primers" instead of their method in setting off the torpedoes.

Credit in this connection is also due Mr. Thomas Weldon, builder of the raft at Snyder's Mills and contractor for the gun boat, at this place for zeal and energy procuring materials for the torpedo party. But this does not take from the merits of Messrs. McDaniel and Ewing for long persistance in their plans under rather discouraging local circumstances. Every assistance asked for by those gentlemen shall be cheerfully given on my part, as has heretofore been done—and when the enemy again attempt to ascend the Yazoo casualties, sudden and severe, may perhaps overtake them—I submit herewith on a separate paper, a written description of the torpedo so used in the destruction of the enemys boat.

I am very respectfully

(signed) I. N. Brown
Commander

(For information of the Navy Department)
The torpedo used by Messrs. McDaniel and Ewing—acting Masters C. S. N.—in the destruction of the enemys gunboat on the Yazoo River, on the 14th December 1862, was a five gallon demijohn (of glass) filled with powder—This demijohn first had a stopper of wax then a plug of India rubber through both of which ran a copper wire 1/16 of an inch in diameter. The wire was made fast to a "friction primer" properly secured inside the demijohn. This wire connected with another torpedo at some distance extending in a direction of crossing the channel. To secure these torpedoes in proper position, a rock or other suitable weight was dropped, having a pulley, or block, with sheare attached, with a line ran—one end of this line was taken a shore, the other made fast to a piece of timber sufficient to float the torpedo which in turn was made fast to the timber by hauling on the shore end of the line the torpedo could be taken to any desired depth.

The water where the enemys boat was destroyed was 35 feet deep. I do not think the torpedoes were more than 6 feet under the water. The explosion occurred by the enemy coming into contact with the wire drawing out the friction tube.

(signed) I. N. B.

Statement of D. M. Currie 10 February 1863

I was engaged in the naval service on the 12th day of December 1862 at the blowing up of the Gun boat Cairo on the Yazoo River and made a drag search the 3rd day after the blowing up. Our boats having been destroyed by the enemy. I saw on the 13 & 14 inst such signs of the blowing up of a boat as to induce the search. Which was on the 3rd day as stated, and as soon as boats could be supplied to make the search. And the day stated, which was the 15th we found the boat and took from her such articles of furniture etc as to convince us that it was the Gun Boat Cairo and she lying in the bottom of the Yazoo River.

We had planted in the River a number of torpedoes under Acting Masters McDaniel and Ewing at the point where the said Gun Boat Cairo lay. So entangled in the wreck as to preclude the posibility of recovery. Our torpedo line was found and after much effort we had to abandon them.

I am familiar with the fact that Z. McDaniel and F. M. Ewing had charge of and superintended the laying of torpedoes in the Yazoo River. And that the said torpedoes destroyed the Gun Boat "Cairo".

Capt. McDaniel was at Vicksburg on the day of the blowing up of said boat, but Capt. Ewing was on the ground at the time of the blowing up of said boat.

I know the fact that the above named parties claim to be the inventors of said torpedoes. the torpedoes were of the following materials, glass demijohns of five gallon size, covered with willow and filled with cannon powder made to act by means of a friction primer.

D. M. Currie

Sworn to and subscribed
before me this 10th day of
February 1863

C. G. Manship
Mayor and ex officio JP

Statement of Charles T. Brooke, 18 February 1863

State of Mississippi
Hinds County

Personally appeared before me Charles T. Brooke and made oath to the following to wit—I was on the Yazoo River on the 12 day of Decbr 1862 the day that the Federal Gun Boat Cairo was sunk, I was in the Naval Service at that time and that the said Gun Boat was destroyed by torpedoes placed there by Z. McDaniel and F. M. Ewing they were acting under and by authority of the Secretary of the Confederate States Navy. I returned to the place next morning where the Gun Boat Cairo was sunk having been kept away that evening by four other Federal gun boats that laid at or near the place until late in the evening of the 12 inst when I returned to the place I found a great deal of the wreck afloat on the surface of the water there being no current in the river to carry it off. I found some tanks, spittoons, hatches, ladders, portfolio letters and a good many discharges of Illinois Volunteers who had been discharged for the purpose of going on the gun boat and a great many things that I did not know what they were among the rest was a peace of timber marked Flag Officer Fort Cairo, and a great many large pieces of timber painted black and looked like peaces of a boat. I then commenced sounding the river and in a short time located the boat in the head of said river she was an iron clad boat—laying right at the point where our torpedoes were located, the buoy line of the torpedoes was under the boat I was convinced of all the examination that I made the Gun Boat Cairo was sunk with torpedoes I know acting master Z. McDaniel and F. M. Ewing had charge of and did place torpedoes in the river at the point where the Gun Boat Cairo was sunk. McDaniel was in Vicksburg on business for the companie. Ewing was on ground in command at the time they claim to be the inventors of said torpedoes, the torpedoes were made of five gallon glass demijohns covered with willow, said boat in my opinion was worth seven hundred thousand dollars she was one of the finest the Federals had on the Mississippi River. I then used grab hooks and dragged up a great many mattresses blankets hammocks and a long anchor chain in all the examination I made I was forced to the conclusion that the Gun Boat Cairo was destroyed by torpedoes that was placed in the river by McDaniel and Ewing.

Charles T. Brooke

Sworn to and subscribed before
me this 18 day of February 1863
Witness my hand and the
seal of the Probate Court
at Office day and date
above written.

R. N. Hale
Probate Clerk

Statement of George B. Stewart and Isaac G. Johnston, 14 February 1863

State of Mississippi
Hinds County

Personally appeared before me George Stewart and made oath to the following facts to wit—(Isaac G. Johnston I was on the Yazoo River on the 12 day of December 1862 the day that the Federal Gun Boat Cairo was sunk. I was in the naval service at that time and that the said gun boat was destroyed by torpedoes placed there by Z. McDaniel and F. M. Ewing. They were acting under and by authority of the Secretary of the Confederate States Navy. I returned to the place next morning having been kept away that evening by four Federal gun boats that layed at or near the place until late in the evening of the 12th inst. When we returned to the place I found a great deal of the reck afloat on the surface of the water. I found some tanks, spittoons, hatches, laders, portfoliers, letters and a great many things that I did not know what they were; among the rest a piece of timber marked Flag Officer Fort Cairo and a great many large pieces of timber that was painted black and looked like pieces of a boat; we then commenced sounding the river and in a short time located the boat in the bend of said river—and I found the bouy line of the torpedoes entangled with the reck and was convinced from all the examination that I made that the gun boat Cairo was sunk with torpedoes. I know that Acting Masters Z. McDaniel and F. M. Ewing had charge of, and did place, torpedoes in the river at the point where the gun boat Cairo was sunk. McDaniel was in Vicksburg on business for the company and Ewing was on the ground at this time. They claimed to be the inventors of said torpedoes. The torpedoes were made of five gallon demijohns, glass covered with willow. I cant approximate the value of said gun boat Cairo, but she had the reputation of being one of the finest boats the Federals had on the Mississippi River. We then used grab, hooks and dragged up a great many mattresses, blankets, hammocks and a long anchor chain—In all the examination that we made we were forced to the conclusion that the gun boat Cairo was destroyed by Torpedoes that were placed in the river by McDaniel and Ewing.

Sworn to and subscribed
before me this 14th February 1863
Z. O. Davis Member of Board of Police

Geo. B. Stewart
Isaac G. Johnston

Statement of T. O. Davis, 25 February 1863

State of Mississippi
Hinds County

This day came T. O. Davis, before me the undersigned and made the following statement, viz: I was on the Yazoo River at the time the Gun Boat Cairo was blown up, at that time I was about a half mile from the place where she was sunk. Our tents were about two or three hundred yards of the place; we had orders to take them down and take care of ourselves as best we could, as we calculated being shelled; as they shelled us before, some of the company went to the hills; about a mile off; I wished to see what they did and went up to the river, about a half mile, when the levy was high so I could hide myself, and have protection from the shells. On the 12th of December last five gun boats and ram came and fortunately the ram Cairo got entangled in one of our torpedoes which blew her up. I heard the torpedo explode; it was quite different from the report of the guns on the boats; I could not see the boat at the time; it was behind the point; there was others in sight firing continually when the torpedo exploded. There was a cloud of white smoke rose above the tops of the trees. I was detailed from the M. M. Minnto to go on the Yazoo River under the command of Z. McDaniel and F. M. Ewing, for the purpose of putting torpedoes in said river. McDaniel and Ewing were acting under authority from this state and perhaps from the Confederate States. They had command of a company for the purpose of putting torpedoes in the Yazoo River as before stated. The Yankees shelled that place till late that day so that we did not visit the place until the next day; we had to get our tents and gather up our goods, that we had scattered in the hurry to get out of the way of the shelling; that kept us till night; next day we went to the place where the boat was sunk, saw the wreck of a boat, drifting on the water; got out a great many things, water tanks, step ladders, spittoons and many other things tedious to mention. Some very long pieces all seamed to be from the inside of the boat. At the point where the boat sunk was a shelving bank and that was torn away seamingly [by] the bow of the boat. I saw when they had carried a large cable round a tree, there was a willow top laying fifteen or twenty or twenty yards from the bank, and in the Water. I said to the man with me that the boat was on that top, for it was out of sight and proposed that we should sound for it. We got a pole with a spike and hook on the end of it and went out in a short time found the wreck ten or twelve feet under water; and in sounding about found a place and got the hook fast to something; after hard pulling, we brought out a hammock, rolled up tight, with a matrass and two blankets in it; after that we got out several more and a large chain about seventy yards long; I am as well satisfied that a torpedo destroyed the Cairo as I am of anything that I did not see. One of the floats that the torpedo was fastened to, was floating triumphantly over the wreck fastened to by one of the ropes, I know that McDaniel and Ewing had charge of and superintended laying of torpedo in said river especially the ones that destroyed the gunboat Cairo. At the time the boat was blown up, Capt. McDaniel had gone to Vicksburg on business; Capt. Ewing was with the company. They are the inventors of the torpedo; they were prepared in camp. As for what this boat cost, I am at a loss to know from what I can see she is large and I think a new boat; Some of the timber that were broken look's to be new. I would think her and fittings did not cost less than five or six hundred thousand dollars.

T. O. Davis

Sworn to and subscribed
before me this 25th Feb, 1863.

State of Mississippi
Hinds Cty

Personally appeared before me Robert N. Hale, Clerk of the Probate Court of said county;, Mr. T. O. Davis who upon oath states that the matters and facts set forth in the forgoing affidavit are true to the best of his knowledge and belief.

Witness my hand and the seal of said court
at office Raymond, February 26, 1863

R. N. Hale, C. K.

Statement of George Work, 17 July 1863

State of Virginia

City of Richmond, to wit:

Capt. Z. McDaniel was at my house at Jackson, Miss in May 1862 and in a few days thereafter, I went into a room and was shown the apparatus he had prepared for the construction of torpedoes and pulleys which I saw in operation, which he insisted with great earnestness would blow up all the vessels of the enemy whenever properly applied. Gov Pettus to whom he was introduced by my wife (while I was at the defence of Vicksburg) immediately had the greatest confidence in him and his torpedoes.

The Governor, myself and the public considered him the sole inventor of the torpedoes which blew up the "Cairo" on the Yazoo River last Decr. The water tank of which was exhibited by the Governor in his office at Jackson with pride and pleasure from that time till taken by the Yankees in May last, other fragments of said boat was in the Governor's office on the day I left 30th inst.

Geo. Work

Subscribed and sworn to before
me this 17th day of July 1863
in the city and state aforesaid.

Alex. H. Sands
Notary Public for Richmond City

Zere McDaniel's Letter to Jefferson Davis, 18 July 1863

Richmond, July 18, 1863

To His Excellency
Jefferson Davis
President of the Confederate States

Sir,

I have the honor to address your Excellency on a subject of vital importance to myself, and of some importance to the Government, insofar as it may effect the good faith of the latter toward its citizens. The subject is the claim presented in the name of McDaniel & Ewing for the destruction of the Federal Gun Boat Cairo. I may *be allowd* to remark in relation to the method by which the Cairo was destroyed, that no part of the invention is due to F. M. Ewing, but that I am the sole inventor and the sole owner of the invention. I invented and contrived the method long before I ever made his acquaintance. He however when the Cairo was destroyed engaged with me in working my invention or method for which I promised to shair with him whatever bounties I might recover from the destruction of vessels with it while we were together operating it. This I intend to do. But he is not a co-inventor with me.

Your Excellency will, I think indulge me, before taking up the more essential merits of my claim and making a brief personal allusion to myself. I am forty-two years old, a native and a citizen of the state of Kentucky before the war a mill right by profession & practice—a vocation which my skill and reputation therein rendered very lucrative, by means whereof I was, when the war commenced, living most easily & Happily with my family in Kentucky where they remain still, cutoff from me; and I was accumulating property which with a large debt due me I left behind when I engaged in the Confederate States. Since I left Kentucky with our Army in February 1862 I have been constantly engaged in the cause; and since then I have encountered every exposure and depravation known to a soldiers life, though not in the regular service until, from being a robust harty man, my constitution is almost completely over throwen, having had chills & fever for the last fifteen months. I invented and constructed the method with which we destroyed the Cairo, early in the spring & summer of 1862, about the months of March, April or May; and with letters of introduction from members of the provisional government of Kentucky under which I had been an officer for the collection of arms etc in that state—Gov Pettus and other gentlemen in Mississippi; I went to Jackson in May 1862 to obtain material & other facilities for making trial and use of my invention. I was kindly received by Gov Pettus and others—and as soon as I got up my material—which was some time in June 1862—I went to the Mississippi river to opperate at Vicksburg. From Vicksburg I went to the Yazoo where I remained and toiled until we destroyed the "Cairo". in January 1861 I went to Port Hudson; in February to Batton Rouge where I made an uncucessful "lick" at the enemys vessls. Whence I went to Franklin, La., and there established there shops to make rope, life-preservers & torpedoes. While then at the request of Gen. Richard Taylor I placed a number of submarine batteries in the Bayou Teche; which detered the enemies Gun Boats and held them of when Gen Taylor had to retreat; and I am satisfied saved the army from capture. In this fight being in the rear with my batteries, while the army was getting away. And having no horses to hall away my tools and materials, I lost evry thing but six locks. After this I went to Gen Braggs army whereby his authority, I have been inventing and opperating a method to destroy the trains of the enemy on the Rail Roads. And just before the retreat from Tullahoma, I destroyed two heavy laden trains between Nashville & Murfresborow. Making total wrecks of them according to the enemys own account.

This have I been constantly employed to subserve the interest of our sacred cause, and in part to serve myself, for I confess that I did desire, and do now desire, if by my ingenuity honestly and patriotically employed I could do sow, to ransom my family from their situation of want in Kentucky, to provide them a comfortable home, and place them above want. And so constanlly thus I have been thus engaged that I have never before last week taken the time to repair to Richmond to look after my claim. I also desire with what the Government ows me in this claim, to obtain means to pay my debts, reimburse my large outlays, and to opperate further with this and other inventions. I know that I can destroy vessels, and Rail Road trains if efficently aided in my exertions, by the government. In my operations with this and my other inventions, the government has rendered me much assistance, by way of furnishing me material, and detailing hands to work with me. But in establishing shops, in paying the wages and board of workmen, and my own personal expences, I have expended all the money I had on hand of my own, and have borrowed of friends large amounts which I have expended, amounting in all to over $20,000, the much larger portion of which was borrowed money. So that if I failed to reciver what is due me in this case I am not only left without my gains and exertion unrewarded but insolvent with a larg debt hanging over me to imbaris all the future opperations of my life.

This much I have thought propir to say by way of inducement to a favorable consideration of my claim. Which I think Your Excellency will again exemin unimbarised by any opinion heretofore formed in regard to it. I will not weary you with a recapitulations of the facts. But will add that my appointment as Acting Master of the Navy was made on the *21st of*

August 1862, fully three months after I had invented my method by which the "Cairo" was destroyed. Everything in regard to my invention, was completed by the midle of May 1862 and even if my invention had of been *after* my appointment, mine was only a temporary appointment given to protect me while I should be at work. So that if I should fall into the hands of the enemy, I would be treated as a prisinor of war and not as a *guerrilla*. A preport of my letter of appointment which I here make, shows this unequivocally, its language bing, "the President has appointed you an Acting Master (temporary for special service in submarine batteries)". Mr. Ewings appointment was made at the same time & of the same character. But I reiterate that the question as to whether an officer of the government may while in government service be a beneficiary under the act of Congress is not an issue in this case, my invention having been made before I even received the temperary and special appointment of Acting Master.

Allow me to call Your Excellencys especial attention to the opinion of the Attorney Generals rendered in my case. Since I understand it was not before you when previously considering this case.

I take it for granted that the originality of my invention or method is sufficiently established, as that has not as yet been questioned, by your Excellency, the Sect of the Navy, or Atty Gen, to all of whom the papers pertaining to my claim have been submitted. The act under which I claim is "an act to amend an act entitled an act, to amend an act to recognize the existance of war & approved by your Excellency April 21st 1862. and is in this language, "That the first Section of the above entitled act, be so amended, that in case any person or persons, shall invent or construct any new machine or engine or construct any new method of destroying the armed vessels of the enemy he or they shall received *fifty percentum* of the value of each and every such vessell that may be sunk or distroyed by means of such invention or contrivance, including the value of the armament thereof in leu of the twenty percentum as provided by said act. (*Sev Act of Congress 1 Sess p 51. als an act Prov Cong 2d Sess p 22, 26 & 85*) This act in all assential respects an independant law, depending on no other for its efficiency or execution, save in so far as the last sentance of the 1st Section of the act of which it is an amendment attaches to it, providing for "The valuation to be made by a board of Naval Officers, appointed and their award to be approved by the President, and the amount found due to be payable in eight percent bonds of the Confederate States" "It is in all other respects an independent law. It has no dependance on the 10th Section of the act of May 6th 1861. for either its construction or execution; And if it had there is nothing in this section to effect either.

Your Excellencys attention is called to additional testimony that of Major George Work of Miss and Senitor John B. Clark of Mo. herewith submited, showing among other things, that my invention or contrivance was prior in time to my appointment. And also to the accompanying printed extract from a letter written soon after the destruction of the "Cairo" by one of its correspondents to the New York Herald showing the admission of the enemy as to the terible and complete effectiveness of my invention and method in the case in question.

Your Excellency will not lose sight of the fact, that my claim is based not upon the fact that we destroyed the "Cairo" but upon the fact that I "invented" or "constructed" the "machine" or "method", by which the vessel was destroyed. I will again call Your Excellencies attention to the opinion of Atty Gen Watts, which sustains fully my claim, boath as to the *law* and the *facts*. In the second paragraph of his opinion he says "it appears by the papers submitted to me that McDaniel & F. M. Ewing *officers* in the *Navy* invented during the year 1862 a submarine battery or torpedo, and constructed several with the appropriate machines attached, and placed them in the Yazoo River in the State of Mississippi, that on or about the 12th day of December last, one of the enemies Gun Boats was by means of this newly invented torpedo battery destroyed". So much for his construction of the facts; as to the *law* in the last paragraph of his opinion he says, "*The facts set fourth in the petition of Messrs McDaniel & Ewing supported by the affidavits submitted to me, brings them within the benefit of this act*. And I *think they are entitled to the bounty therein provided. And a board of naval Officers to value the sunken or destroyed vessel, including the armament*."

Here is the opinion of the chief law officer of the Government, clearly and unequivocally endorsing my claim, both as to *law*, and *fact*—eaven suposing us to be officers when I invented or contrivd my machine or method. Now that I have established clearly, that I invented or contrived my machine or method before I became a *qualified* officer, I think Your Excellency will no longer hesitate to award me the board of Naval Officers to make the valuation as required by the act of Congress, which has encouraged me as well as others to exert my inventive genius for the destruction of the enemys vessels. That we destroyed the Cairo with my invention or contrivance there can be no kind of question. It knocked a hole in her bottom, "from six to eight feet in length and very scraggy. Water poured in at a terrible rate, and it was at once apparent, there was no hopes of saving the vessel," and "in seven minutes from the time the torpedo exploded beneath her the "Cairo" went down in six fathums water, *nothing whatever* being saved but her officers & crew, her magniffi-cent battery of thirteen heavy guns, with her well stored magazine, together with her engine & boilers, and all her furniture, with the personal effects of her officers and crew, are a totle and irrecoverable loss." I will not so much infring the good faith of the government as to dwell on this presentation of facts, that the manifist justice and legality of my claim, will be at once be recognized, and justice a warded. If mine is not a clear case under the law, I submit most respectfully, that the law ought to be repealed, that others may not be induced by it jeopardize their lives to say nothing of health, with dangerous experiments, and to expend large sums of money, with the expectation that their success shall be rewarded as the law prescribes, when their only requital is to be a mortifying disappointment, if not injustice, but with abiding confidince in your Excellencis clear preception of law and justice I rest our case.

Respectfully Submitted
Z. McDaniel

The Thomas Weldon Claim, Undated

To the Honble Congress of the C. S.

Your petitioner begs leave to submit herewith, accompanying papers, showing that he caused the destruction of the property of the public enemy, caused by the blowing up of the U. S. Gunboat Cairo, in the Yazoo river, state of Mississippi on or about the 12th of December A.D. 1862. and to solicit such reward for the service as your honorable body may think deserved by the service.

Respectfully
Thos. Weldon

Statement of John Beggs, 23 March 1864

Demopolis, Ala March 23, 1864
Mr. Thos. Weldon

Sir

In reply to your request of me to give you a correct statement in reference to the destruction of the U.S. Gunboat Cairo which was sunk in the Yazoo River in 1862 by torpedoes. The facts in relation to the sinking of the vessel are as follows. The apparatus used by Mr. Z. McDaniel would not answer the purpose or had failed to ignite the powder on every attempt made. Mr. Burton was sent by Commander I. N. Brown of the CSN to assist us in the operation. After several unsuccessful trials Burton supposed further attempts useless and left for Yazoo City but he returned the second day following with the materials which you had purchased in Vicksburg and some friction primers which he stated you had obtained from Col. Higgins. And together with the materials referred to, the torpedoes were made by which the Cairo was sunk. I was with Mr. Z. McDaniel from the 11th of Nov 1862 until the 27th of April 1863 after the destruction was effected by your invention and assistance rendered by you. Myself and Mr. Tucker placed the torpedoes in the river. The first was exploded by the hands of Tucker and Sprawls and had by little effect—the next was exploded by the vessel coming in contact with them and by wich the Cairo was sunk. Mr. Z. McDaniel was in Vicksburg at the time of its occurrence.

Yours very respectfully,
John Beggs

State of Alabama
Marengo County

This day John Beggs personally appeared before the undersigned Justice of the Peace in and for the county aforesaid and being duly sworn he deposeth and saith that the foregoing statement signed by himself is just true and correct in every particular to the best of his knowledge & belief.

Sworn to and subscribed before
me this 11th May 1864

Geo. E. Markham, JP
Marengo County, Ala

Statement of Edward C. Blake, 26 March 1864

Selma, Ala   March 26, 1864

Col. Thomas Weldon

Sir,

In reference to the sinking of the U.S. Gunboat Cairo of which you request me to give you a correct statement. The circumstances are as follows. Mr. Burton stated to you in my presence at Snyder's Bluff where I was assisting you in making obstructions for the Yazoo River that he was ordered by Commander Brown to ascertain why the enemy could pass the torpedoes which Mr. McDaniel had been placing in the river without being injured by them and if possible to make them effective. After the elaps of several days, Burton returned to the bluff and stated that there was no hope of success in consequence of the deficiency of the torpedoes and that further attempts to injure the enemy should be a waste of time and that he was going to Yazoo City to report to Commander Brown. You then expressed your belief that it was practicable to make a torpedo by which the enemy could be injured stating at the same time that you were going to Vicksburg to procure materials for the purpose and requested Burton to go with you which he did. You returned with the materials the night following and got some friction primers from Col. Higgins and on the next day you directed me to make some nessary appliances and go with Burton for the purpose of trying your torpedo. Your orders were immediately put in execution and the first approach of the enemy two of the torpedoes were exploded by means of a laniard from the shore—which produced no effect other than causing the gunboats to withdraw. You then [dir]ected placing them in that the explosion would be made by the vessel which was done and on the return of the gunboats one of them was sunk by two of your torpedoes. McDaniel was absent at the time of the occurrence. At the approach of the enemy we retired to a camp which was out of range of the guns. McDaniel returned to the camp that evening and stated that he had been to Vicksburg ordering some locks without which he said we could do nothing. Both he and Ewing expressed much disapprobation of your plan;. We were all as yet ignorant of what had been done. On the next day we went to the river and found you and Capt. Shepperd their examining the floating wreck and then found that a gunboat had been sunk which was afterwards reported to be the Cairo. I am aware that McDaniel was anxious that you would claim a reward from the government for sinking her in order that all concerned in the matter might share in a portion of it. I mention his injections to you in reference to making the claim. Your reply was that your object was not to involve your government in cost, but to injure that of the enemy.

Edward C. Blake

Sworn to and Subscribed
the 19th May 1864 before me
[Illegible] J.P.

Colonel Edward Higgins's Letter to Weldon, 6 May 1864

Selma May 6th 1864

I was in command of the troops which were stationed at Snyder's Bluff on the Yazoo River—December 1862. when the Federal gun boat "Cairo" was destroyed by a torpedo. and I have every reason to believe that the destruction of that vessel was occasioned by the injenious arrangement of Mr. Thomas Weldon who succeeded by the use of friction primer in producing an explosion when other methods had failed. Mr. Weldon applied to me for material which was furnished by my order and for the purpose of enabling him to test fully on the enemy the value of the torpedo as an offensive weapon.

Edward Higgins
Brig Genl CSA

Official
Gaston Meolier
Aide de Camp

Thomas Weldon's Letter to Isaac N. Brown, 12 May 1864

Demopolis, Alabama May 12, 1864

Commander I. N. Brown
C.S. Navy
Charleston Harbour
S.C.

Sir,

I had the honor to receive your message by Mr. Colter informing me that a claim for sinking the United States Gunboat "Cairo" had been laid before the Department and would be paid.

Mr. Colter informed me that you had notified the Department that Mr. Burton and myself were entitled to a portion of whatever might be awarded.

The facts concerning the matter (of which I believe you are cognizant) are as follows: the apparatus used by Mr. McDaniel failed to be effective. Mr. Burton whom you sent to assist him, informed me of this failure at Snyder's Bluff, where I was engaged in obstructing the Yazoo River. He was on his way to report to you at Yazoo City and had abandoned all hopes of success.

Believing myself that an efficient torpedo could be made, I requested Mr. Burton to accompany me to Vicksburg to procure, if possible, material for the purpose which was accomplished on the day following, at my own expense we returned to Snyder's Bluff the same night, and with some friction primers, which I obtained from Colonel Edward Higgins, and other materials brought from Vicksburg a torpedo was arranged; by two of which the "Cairo" was sunk. On the first trial the explosion was made by hand with but little effect; the next was by contact of the vessel and effective.

I beg leave to assert that I was not actuated by the expectation of personal gain to embark in this enterprise; but with the hope of performing what I conceived to be my duty to my country, its posterity, and my God.

As the matter however has been brought to the attention of the Government, and a remuneration for its success required by persons who do not deserve it, I have determined to present you with this statement of the facts in the case, in order that, if there is any honor or award to be rendered, it may induce the government to bestow it upon those justly entitled to it.

As you are familiar with the parties, and probably with those facts, permit me to rely upon your assistance to have retained whatever portion Mr. Burton and myself are entitled to, in the event any payment being proposed. Accept my thanks for your kind consideration, and allow me, Commander, to remain,

Respectfully
Your obedient servant,
Thos. Weldon

Statement of facts concerning the sinking of the U.S. Gunboat Cairo upon which the opinion of Commander I. N. Brown, CSN, is respectfully solicited.

Charleston, May 19, 1864

Respectfully returned for the use of Mr. Thos. Weldon whose statement regarding the part performed by himself and Mr. Burton in the destruction of the U.S.S. Cairo agrees with all the information official and otherwise that I had at the time of the affair taking place. In my official report of which I called the attention of the Navy Department to the valuable aid rendered by Mr. Weldon and Mr. Burton. Stating also that credit was due to Messrs. McDaniel and Ewing for having originated the attempts to destroy the enemys gunboats by torpedoes on the Yazoo River.

I. N. Brown
Commr, CSN

Statement of Francis Marion Tucker, 16 May 1864

Mobile, May 16th, 1864

Thos. Weldon

Sir: The following is a correct [state]ment of the facts connected with the sinking [of the] Federal gunboat Cairo, which was sunk [on] the Yazoo River on the twelfth day of [Dec]ember A.D. 1862 by torpedoes.

Z. McDaniel prepaired some torpedoes on [the Yazoo] missing entirely from those by which Cairo was destroyed. His torpedoes were placed [in] the river below where you were obstructing it at Snyders Bluff. I superintended the placing of them. His torpedoes would not answer the intended purpose. Genl. Smith who was in command at Vicksburg at that time, expressed much dissatisfaction with our operations. Mr. Burton came to assist us as he stated by order of Capt. Brown of the C.S.N. After his arrival several unsuccessful attempts were made to remedie the cause of their failure. Burton [returned to report to] Capt. Brown. After two days absence he returned bringing with him various materials which he stated you had purchased at Vicksburg for the purpose of trying a torpedo on a plan of your own. He also brought some friction primers, which he stated you had obtained from Col. Higgins, who was then in command at Snyder's Bluff.

A carpenter by the name of Bl[ake] [was] with Burton whom he stated you [sent] to assist in the operation.

With the primers and materials [which] you sent, some torpedoes were [made] on your plan.

On the first approach of the enemy gunboats, two of them was expl[oded] [illegible] by Mr. Sprowls & myself. The explosion was effected by means of lines or wires leading from the torpedo to shore. By these torpedoes the enemy received no injury, but went back. The next was placed so as to explode by contact of the vessel and by them the Cairo was sunk.

McDaniel was opposed to this plan. He left for Vicksburg before the occurrance and did not return until evening after the Cairo was sunk.

Much was said in reference to the [torpedoes. McDaniel] expressed his belief that [your] plan would not answer.

Ewing stated that he would have nothing more to do with the torpedoes.

The next day he went to the river and found some floating pieces of gun boat. Yourself and [Lt. She]pperd of the C.S.N. was there [ex]amining a boat was found sunk. I was with McDaniel [from] the commencement of his operations [o]n the Yazoo River until the time [of this] occurrence. Your torpedoes by which [the] Cairo was sunk was placed in the river by [myself], John Beggs, Mr. Sprawls and two others who[se names] I don't

[know]. M[cDaniel] did not assist in any arrangement of these [torpedoes].

Respectfully yours,
X His mark
Francis Marion Tucker
Attest J. R. Eastburn

The State of Alabama
Mobile County

I J. R. Eastburn, a notary public of said county and state herebty certify that Francis Marion Tucker whose name is signed in the foregoing instrument of writing and who is known to me acknowledge [illegible]

the 16th day of May A. D. 1864

J. R. Eastburn
Notary Public Mobile County
Alabama

Statement of David Curry, 4 July 1864

Clinton LA July 4, 1864

Col. Thos. Weldon

Sir. I give you the following statement of the facts concerning the sinking of a federal gunboat which was sunk by torpedoes in the Yazoo River in the month of December 1862. Mr. Z. McDaniel was operating in the Yazoo River with torpedoes. I was assisting him in doing so before and after the destruction of the Cairo. His torpedoes were arranged with a tube extending from the chamber in which the powder was contained. This tube was incased in a wooden box within which was a lock similar to that of a gun. The trigger could be worked by wires. Ignition was to be effected by a percussion cap. The case around the tube could not be made water tight. Therefore, the powder became wet in a short time after being submerged and his torpedoes invariable failed [in] opperation. Previous to the destruction of the Cairo Mr. Burton came to assist us as he stated by order of Commander I. N. Brown of the C.S.N. After the arrival of Burton, several attempts were made to get McDaniel's torpedoes to ignite, which they failed to do. Burton then left as he stated to report the plan a failure. On the second day following, he returned in company with a carpenter whose name I think was Blake. They brought with them white lead, wax, tallows, gutta percha, ropes, wire, friction primers, weights for anchors, pulleys and a lot of demijohns etc all of which Burton stated had been purchased by you at Vicksburg for the purpose of trying torpedoes upon a plan of your own which was immediately done in the following manner. The powder was put into the demijohn. the primer was inserted in a wooden shaft. This shaft extended in the powder to below the center. Its top end came a small distance up the neck of the demijohn. A groove was cut in the side of the shaft for the wires which was attached to the primers and forced through the gum extending some distance outside of the demijohn. To this wire would be attached a line or wire. The gum was fitted tight into the neck of the demijohn, one piece resting on the top of the shaft. On this was poured melted wax. The neck was then nearly filled with tallow. On top of this was fitted another piece of gum which was well secured by means of wires bound round the neck of the demijohn and lashed over the top of the gum. In [securing] them weights were used for anchors by which means, with the ropes and pulleys they were drawn under water to any required depth. The first trial two of them were exploded at the gunboats of the enemy, one of them by Mr. Sprawls and one by Mr. Tucker. These done the enemy no damage.

You then proposed to place them so as to be exploded by the vessel which was done. By this means and with two of your torpedoes, the Cairo was sunk. McDaniel was at Vicksburg when the vessel was sunk. He returned to camp that evening which was some distance from the river. He stated that nothing could be effected by your plan. Ewing swore that he would have no further connection with torpedoes. No one at camp knew the vessel had been sunk until the next day when we went to the River. Capt. Shepperd and yourself was there with a boat and found the wreck [close by where] the torpedoes were placed in the river. I was with McDaniel for some time after the Cairo was sunk during which time he proposed many projects some of which he tried but without any success.

Respectfully yours etc
David Curry

Statement of James J. Dees, 5 July 1864

Clinton, LA July 5, 1864

Col. Thos. Weldon

Sir, in reference to the yankey gunboat Cairo which was sunk by torpedoes in the Yazoo River in December 1862.

I can stated that I was attached to a company which was organized by Mr. Z. McDaniel for the purpose of operating against the vessels of the enemy by means of torpedoes. Those used by him were constructed with a pipe leading from the apartment which contained the powder into a wooden box in which was placed a lock like the lock of a gun to which was attached wires by means of which the lock could be set and the trigger worked by this method with a percussion cap the powder was to be ignited in consequence of some *deficiency* his powder became wet and could not be ignited. Sometime previous to the sinking of the Cairo a man by the name of Burton came to assist us he stated that he was ordered to do so by Capt. Brown of the C.S.N. He endeavored to get McDaniels torpedoes to answer but could not succeede he then left and said he would report them as a failure in about two days from the time he left he returned again in company with a carpenter I think his name was Blake they brought with them a quantity of materials of various kinds which Burton stated was purchased by you at Vicksburg with thies materials torpedoes were made upon a plan proposed by you and entirely different from those made by McDaniel his being ignited by means of a percussion cap and yours by means of a friction primer his powder being in a tin can with a pipe as described and yours being in a demijohn your torpedoes were first tried by pulling wires from the shore the first was pulled by Messrs. Sproul and Tucker from which the enemy received no injury the next were placed so that the wire was pulled by the vessel and by those the Cairo was sunk McDaniel was absent when the vessel was sunk the same evening he returned to camp that day when the gunboats came up all the company left the river and came to the camp which was about one mile from the river Ewing was much dissatisfied and wished to be considered as having nothing more to do with the torpedoes both him and McDaniel expressed their confidence that your plan would not answer all were ignorant of the vessel being sunk until the next day when the wreck was discovered I was with McDaniel from October 1862 until the fifth of January 1863 at which time he left the Yazoo River after which I believe he went to Port Hudson, La to operate upon the Mississippi River.

Respectfully yours etc
James J. Dees

Statement of John C. Stancil, 11 September 1864

Tom Big Bee Gunboat Landing
September 11, 1864

Mr. Weldon since Mr. Blake tells me that you wished to see me concerning McDaniel and the destruction of the Yanky gun boat Cairo in the Yazoo River what I have to say about it McDaniels plans never destroyed the boat for I was an artificer in company all the time his plans never would work it was by your plans that the boat was destroyed therefore I would testify that he was not entitle one cent McDaniel was drunk in Vicksburg the day the boat was blown up and Ewing was the first man left run through the swamp and reported me captured because I did not leave as soon as the crowd did If there is any information you wish relative to the matter you will address me Tom Big Bee gunboat landing care J. M. LeeBaron, Mobile, Ala. I remain yours etc

John C. Stancil

Notes

Abbreviations

MA Mississippi State Archives, Jackson, Mississippi
NA National Archives and Records Administration, Washington, D.C.
RG Record Group
ORA *U.S. War Department. The War of the Rebellion: A Compilation of the Official Records of the Union and Confederate Armies*. 70 vol. in 128 vols. Washington, D.C.: U.S. Government Printing Office, 1880–1901.
ORN U.S. Navy Department. *Official Records of the Union and Confederate Navies in the War of the Rebellion*. 30 vols. Washington, D.C.: U.S. Government Printing Office, 1894–1914.

The majority of the records concerning the McDaniel-Ewing claim and the Weldon claim for the sinking of the USS *Cairo* are located in Vessel Papers C-225, USS *Cairo*, Record Group 45, National Archives. For simplicity in the notes, the entry C225, NA, designates that location. Francis M. Ewing's statement constitutes the body of the initial McDaniel-Ewing claim. Typescript copies of all known claim documents available are found in the Appendix of this book.

Chapter 1: *Constantly Engaged in the Cause*

1. Zere McDaniel to Jefferson Davis, July 18, 1863, C225, NA. McDaniel registered at least three patents. His first was patent number 30 025 filed with the United States Patent Office September 11, 1860, for a new method of hanging millstones. His second was a patent for torpedoes with the Confederate Patent Office, number 198, September 8, 1863. Its description is unknown. His third was a patent for torpedoes, Confederate Patent Office, number 202, September 21, 1863. His United States patent is recorded in the United States Patent and Trademark Office. His Confederate patent number 202 is currently in the possession of the Confederate museum in Richmond, Virginia. See Records of the Clerk of the

Circuit Court, Deed Book M, p. 145, September 16, 1860 microfilm 978016), Allen County Public Library, Scottsville, Kentucky. McDaniel sold the right to sell his patented method of hanging millstones in one-fourth of the territory of Ohio and one-half the state of Indiana to R. L. Brown and others. Also see Francis A. Lord, *Civil War Collector's Encyclopedia* (Secaucus, N.J.: Castle, 1982), pp. 351–53, for a listing of all Confederate patents, including McDaniel's, in a report by Confederate Patent Commissioner Rufus S. Rhodes.

2. McDaniel's first name was given in many variations during his life. The few official legal documents record it as Zere, but it is Zera in a partial biography of his daughter Quinlinnia McDaniel Weir, in Thomas W. Westerfield, ed., *Kentucky Genealogy and Biography*, 2 vols. (Owensboro, Ky.: Genealogical Reference Company, 1971), 2:72, as follows: "a daughter of Zera and Elizabeth C. (Berry) McDaniel, who were born respectively in Georgia and Barren County, Kentucky. Zera McDaniel was a skilled mechanic and invented numerous patents and torpedoes about the close of the late Rebellion." McDaniel gave his place of birth as Virginia in the 1860 Kentucky census, Barren County, p. 1059, in which he was enumerated with George Cake's family.

3. Records of the Barren County Court of Equity and Criminal Matters, Deed Book 2, p. 200, 1861, in Office of the Clerk of the Barren County Circuit Court, Glasgow, Kentucky.

4. *Louisville Daily Journal*, January 25, 1862, p. 2, col. 3. Also see Frank Moore, ed., *The Rebellion Record*, 4 vols. (New York: G. P. Putnam, 1862–66), 4:12.

5. *Louisville Daily Journal*, September 25, 1862, p. 2, col. 3; Barren County Equity and Criminal Court, Order Book 22, p. 51, in Office of the Barren County Circuit Court, Glasgow, Kentucky, September 12, 1864, shows that McDaniel was indicted by the Unionist government of Kentucky for treason. On September 10, 1864, McDaniel was indicted for usurpation of office (ibid., p. 44).

6. McDaniel to Davis, July 18, 1863.

7. Ibid., Statement of George Work, July 17, 1863, C225, NA.

8. The explosive devices that we today know as naval mines went by several names during the Civil War. They were called torpedoes, submarine batteries, and infernal machines. They were named torpedoes after a suborder of the family of stingrays, *Torpedinoidei*, called electric rays or torpedo fish, elliptical or oval-shaped rays that use electric current pods on their bodies (measured as high as two hundred volts and two thousand watts) to stun other aquatic animals that come into direct contact with them. They are found on the Atlantic Coast of the United States as well as parts of European waters.

9. Statement of Work; McDaniel to Davis, July 18, 1863.

10. McDaniel to Pettus, June 5, 1862, telegram, Administration of Governor John J. Pettus, Telegrams Received, vol. 55, RG 27, MA. During the Civil War the term, *batteries* in this context meant submarine batteries, not electrical batteries. Electrical batteries were called galvanic cells.

11. Alfred Thayer Mahan, *The Gulf and Inland Waters* (New York: Charles Scribner's Sons, 1883), p. 46.

12. McDaniel to Davis, July 18, 1863.

13. David D. Porter, *Naval History of the Civil War* (1886; rpt. Secaucus, N.J.: Castle, 1984), p. 249; J. Thomas Scharf, *History of the Confederate States Navy* (1887; rpt. New York: Fairfax Press, 1977), p. 310.

14. Samuel Carter III, *The Final Fortress* (1980; rpt. Wilmington, N.C.: Broadfoot Press, 1988), p. 69.

15. Ibid., p. 71; Porter, *Naval History*, p. 260.

16. His contact with Isaac N. Brown may have been the source of McDaniel's entry into the Torpedo service. Brown was at New Orleans in early 1862 and went to Vicksburg after the city fell in April.

17. Carter, *Final Fortress*, pp. 91–92. Carter cites Isaac Brown's "Confederate Torpedoes in the Yazoo" in Robert U. Johnson and Clarence C. Buel, eds., *Battles and Leaders of the Civil War*, 4 vols. (New York: Century, 1887–88), 3:580, as his source for Kennon's claim and mentions the galvanic cell theory of detonation for the torpedo that sank the *Cairo*. Brown's article does not mention Kennon or the use of electrically fired torpedoes against the *Cairo*. He describes only the use of friction primers. Scharf, *History of the Confederate States Navy*, p. 752, notes Kennon's claim that he trained McDaniel in August 1862 but correctly states that the torpedo the *Cairo* hit was detonated with a friction primer.

18. McDaniel to Pettus, June 5, 1862, telegram; Statement of Work; McDaniel to Davis, July 18, 1863.

19. Richard L. Maury, *A Brief Sketch of the Work of Matthew Fontaine Maury during the War, 1861–1865* (Richmond: Whittet & Shepperson, 1915), p. 16.

20. U.S. War Department, *Military Law and Precedents* by William Winthrop, 2d ed. (Washington, D.C.: U.S. Government Printing Office, 1920), p. 769: "And so one who comes secretly within the lines with a view to the destruction of property, killing of persons, robbery and the like is not as such a spy." He mentions in a footnote that John Y. Beall, Confederate secret agent, was wrongly executed as a spy when, in reality, he was a violator of the law of war as a "prowler" or guerrilla. In discussing guerrillas (p. 783), he says that they "are not in general recognized as legitimate troops or entitled, when taken, to be treated as prisoners of war, but may upon capture be summarily punished even with death." The letter of appointment is Stephen R. Mallory to Flag Officer William F. Lynch, August 22, 1862, C225, NA.

21. William S. Dudley, Assistant Head, Historical Research Branch, Naval Historical Center, to author, June 20, 1978.

22. Index to Confederate Soldiers from Mississippi, Roll 12, E, NA microfilm 232. Ewing is shown as an independent private, in the Twelfth Mississippi Regiment and also, apparently later, "Clerk, Treasury Department," presumably meaning the Treasury Department of the Confederate government. In the McDaniel-Ewing Claim, C225, NA, Ewing states that he "has served as an independent Private with the Raymond Fancibles [sic] 12th Miss. Regiment for 15 months. he had previously lost his right arm—but fought with a breech loading Maynard rifle supported by a shoulder strap. He received for this service no pay." See also P. L. Rainwater, ed., "W. A. Montgomery's Record of the Raymond Fencibles," *Journal of Mississippi History* 6 (1944):113. The Raymond Fencibles were designated Com-

pany A, Twelfth Mississippi Infantry Regiment. Ewing's name is not among the members listed by Rainwater.

23. Porter, *Naval History*, p. 250.

24. *Atlas to Accompany the Official Records of the Union and Confederate Armies* (Washington, D.C.: U.S. Government Printing Office, 1891–95), Plate XXVII, #2.

25. Goodspeed Company, *Biographical and Historical Memoirs of Mississippi*, 2 vols. (Chicago: Goodspeed Company, 1891), 1:328. Weldon is also listed in the 1860 Mississippi census at Jefferson County, p. 48. He is shown as age forty-nine and a "master mechanic." Interview with Gordon Cotton, Curator, Old Courthouse Museum, Vicksburg, Mississippi, September 27, 1991.

26. Joseph N. Kane, *Famous First Facts* (New York: H. W. Wilson, 1964), p. 624.

27. Allen Johnson and Dumas Malone, eds., *Dictionary of American Biography* (New York: Charles Scribner's Sons, 1928–77), 7:70, 8:263.

28. Maury, *Brief Sketch*, pp. 7, 14.

29. "Batteries," *Encyclopedia Americana*, 30 vols. (Danbury, Conn.: Grolier, 1985), 3:358.

30. Maury, *Brief Sketch*, p. 13. See also Burke Davis, *The Civil War: Strange and Fascinating Facts* (New York: Fairfax Press, 1982), p. 107, who attributes the story of the lack of insulated cable, the washing up of insulated electric cable in the Chesapeake, and the spies to the north to Gabriel J. Raines. See also R. O. Crowley, "The Confederate Torpedo Service," in Philip Van Doren Stern, ed., *Secret Missions of the Civil War* (New York: Rand McNally, 1959), pp. 207–12.

31. Maury, *Brief Sketch*, p. 12.

32. Scharf, *History of the Confederate States Navy*, p. 306.

33. *ORN*, Ser. I, vol. 22, p. 791. Maury's subsequent letter to Polk re: "Submarine batteries," ibid., p. 806.

34. Ibid., pp. 651, 806–7; Milton F. Perry, *Infernal Machines: The Story of Confederate Submarine and Mine Warfare* (Baton Rouge: Louisiana State University Press, 1965), pp. 10-12.

35. Davis, *Civil War*, pp. 105–9; Stewart Sifakis, *Who Was Who in the Civil War* (New York: Facts on File, 1988), p. 528; J. W. Minnich, "Incidents of the Penninsula Campaign," *Confederate Veteran* 30 (February 1922): 53. Minnich, of Hampton's Legion, relates how Raines provided guides for Confederate forces to allow them to traverse mine fields at night. Also see *ORA*, Ser. I, vol. 28, pt. 2, pp. 371–72, for a letter from Raines to Seddon concerning the use of subterra shells to stop cavalry raids.

36. Jefferson Davis, *The Rise and Fall of the Confederate Government*, 2 vols. (New York: D. Appleton, 1881), 2:208.

37. Crowley, "Confederate Torpedo Service," pp. 210–11, 218.

38. Ibid., p. 210.

39. Friction primers were in use even aboard the USS *Cairo*. Some were recovered from the wreck and are on display at the *Cairo* exhibit, Vicksburg National Military Park.

40. Albert Manucy, *Artillery through the Ages* (Washington, D.C.: U.S. Government Printing Office, 1949), pp. 26–27.

41. U.S. War Department, *The Ordnance Manual for Use by the Officers of the United States Army*, 3d ed. (Philadelphia: J. P. Lippincott, 1862), p. 298.
42. Ibid., p. 242.

CHAPTER 2: *A Torpedo Exploded and Tore the Boat Fearfully*

1. David D. Porter, *Naval History of the Civil War* (1886; rpt. Secaucus, N.J.: Castle, 1984), p. 138. The Western Flotilla was manned by soldiers commanded by naval officers. See Howard P. Nash, Jr., *A Naval History of the Civil War* (Cranbury, N.J.: A. S. Barnes, 1972), p. 29.
2. Porter, *Naval History*, p. 284.
3. Ulysses S. Grant, *Personal Memoirs*, 2 vols. (New York: Charles L. Webster, 1885), 1:430–31.
4. *ORN*, Ser. I, vol. 2, pp. 495, 515–17, 688–89.
5. Ibid., pp. 534, 689.
6. Mark M. Boatner III, *The Civil War Dictionary*, rev. ed. (New York: David McKay, 1988), pp. 820–21. Boatner's estimates from U.S. Naval Observatory data are based on the difference between beginning of morning nautical twilight (BMNT) and the end of evening nautical twilight (EENT). Nautical twilight is the condition which will allow observation and identification of objects on the ground at a distance of four hundred yards. It is commonly used in the military to denote that time at which military operations can be conducted during daylight and, until the advent of night vision equipment, dictated the beginning and end of many daily military operations.
7. Statement of David Curry, July 4, 1864; Statement of James J. Dees, July 5, 1864, both in C225, NA.
8. *ORN*, Ser. I, vol. 25, p. 545.
9. Statement of T. O. Davis, February 25, 1863, C225, NA. Davis said he had been "detailed from the M. M. Minnto to go on the Yazoo River under the command of Z. McDaniel and F. M. Ewing, for the purpose of putting torpedoes in said river."
10. Ibid. There exist two letters with different spellings of the name. D. M. Currie provided a statement for McDaniel's claim, and David Curry wrote a statement to Thomas Weldon in support of Weldon's claim. The signatures do not appear to be the same. D. M. Currie is possibly the thirty-two-year-old Mississippi-born farmer from Jackson, Hinds County, Mississippi, listed in the 1860 Census, Hinds County, p. 539.
11. Stuart may be George B. Stewart, a thirty-six-year-old Mississippi-born farmer from Auburn, Hinds County, Mississippi (1860 Census, Hinds County, p. 611).
12. Brooke is possibly Charles T. Brooke, the nineteen-year-old eldest son of Walker Brooke from Warren County, Mississippi (1860 Census, Warren County, p., 48).
13. Davis is possibly T. O. Davis, a forty-two-year-old Scottish-born farmer from Auburn, Hinds County, Mississippi (1860 Census, Hinds County, p. 697).
14. Beggs was probably John Beggs, a Scottish-born twenty-three-year-old

gunsmith from Port Gibson, Claiborne County, Mississippi (1860 Census, Claiborne County, p. 495).

15. Dees was probably James J. Dees, a thirty-one-year-old Alabama-born farmer from Terry's Depot, Hinds County, Mississippi (1860 Census, Hinds County, p. 655).

16. Sprawls was possibly Samuel Sprawls, a forty-three-year-old planter from Yazoo County, Mississippi (1860 Census, Yazoo County, p. 1019). The name is sometimes spelled Sprouls.

17. Stancil was possibly John C. Stancil of Blount County, Alabama (1860 Census, Blount County, p. 962).

18. Statement of Francis Marion Tucker, May 16, 1864, C225, NA.

19. Burton left no apparent record of his involvement, but many documents mention him. The only record I found of him is in "Reference Cards Related to Papers Relating to Naval Personnel, A–G," reel 5, microfilm M260, RG9, MA, which contains a voucher, no. 24, in which Burton signed for two coils of rope from the Vicksburg post quartermaster, Captain Thomas, on January 27, 1863.

20. Statement of Edward C. Blake, March 26, 1864, C225, NA.

21. Ibid.

22. Statement of Curry. Curry's is the most complete description of the construction of the torpedo available.

23. Alfred Thayer Mahan, *The Gulf and Inland Waters* (New York: Charles Scribner's Sons, 1883), pp. 117–18.

24. The *Baron de Kalb* was the former *St. Louis*. When control of the Mississippi Squadron was transferred from the army to the navy, the navy discovered that it already had a *St. Louis* in inventory so the city-class ironclad *St. Louis* was renamed *Baron DeKalb*.

25. The Ellet rams were not part of the Western Flotilla but an independent army ram fleet (Nash, *Naval History*, p. 29). They went pretty much where they wanted to go and attached themselves to the Western Flotilla for duty as required. Although Sutherland placed his boat temporarily under Walke's command, his actual commander was Colonel Charles R. Ellet.

26. *ORN*, Ser. I, vol. 25, p. 546; Statement of Tucker; Statement of John Beggs, March 23, 1864, C225, NA.

27. Statements of Tucker, Beggs (who reported that he and Tucker placed the torpedoes in the river and that they were exploded "by the hands of Tucker and Sprouls and had but little effect"), and Dees.

28. Statements of Tucker and Blake (Blake, according to his letter and others, had returned with Burton to the lower quarter and seems to have been present on December 11); Mahan, *Gulf and Inland Waters*, p. 118.

29. *ORN*, Ser. I, vol. 25, p. 546. A rifle ball striking the glass demijohn would break the glass, allowing water to rush in and render the black powder ineffective. The only detonating mechanism was the friction primer, and if a rifle ball accidentally hit the primer after passing through the glass casing, the volume of water was such that no detonation would likely occur. We know now that both torpedoes fired that day were intentionally detonated by Tucker and Sprawls.

30. Ibid., p. 547.

31. McDaniel-Ewing Claim, March 23, 1863, C225, NA.

32. All of Weldon's statements mention or list the supplies brought by Burton to McDaniel's camp, but there is no mention of cannon powder, and McDaniel's request indicates that it was not readily available to the torpedo crew.

33. Administration of Governor John J. Pettus, Telegrams Received, 1861–63, vol. 55, RG 27, MA.

34. The McDaniel-Ewing claim, the supporting statements for both claims, and the letters to Weldon all note that McDaniel was in Vicksburg on company business and Ewing was left in command on the river. Statement of John C. Stancil, September 11, 1864, C225, NA, declared that "McDaniel was drunk in Vicksburg the day the boat was blown up and Ewing was the first man left run through the swamp." No other source corroborates Stancil's derogation of McDaniel and Ewing.

35. Report of R. W. Sutherland to Colonel Charles Rivers Ellet, December 12, 1862, from the Mississippi River, Area 5 Files, Ellet Papers, RG 45, N.A.

36. *ORN*, Ser. I, vol. 25, pp. 546–47.

37. Ibid., pp. 551, 545.

38. Ibid., p. 553. Clearly, Walke cautioned his commanders about the danger involved.

39. Ibid., pp. 546, 551, 548 50. Only once in his report to Porter did Walke mention "the ram *Queen of the West*, whose commander desired to *accompany* the expedition" (ibid., p. 553). Sutherland even says, "I *accompanied* the late expedition up the Yazoo River" (Sutherland to Ellet, December 12, 1862); emphasis added.

40. Ibid., pp. 547, 553. Fentress said that Williams and Blake were picked up at 10:00 A.M. Getty thought it was about one-half hour before they arrived at the torpedoes, which was estimated to be about noon.

41. McDaniel-Ewing Claim; Statements of Davis and Blake.

42. The following description of the Union actions is taken from the eyewitness statements of the commanders of the various Union vessels in *ORN*, Ser. I, vol. 25, pp. 544–56.

43. Ibid., p. 554. Fentress risked the safety of the *Marmora* and her crew by taking the torpedo on board. An explosion could have occurred, killing or wounding those nearby and possibly causing structural damage to the ship. Fentress may have assumed that the torpedoes were electrically detonated and cutting the line made them safe. Sutherland reported that "the *Cairo* moved forward a short distance in the middle of the stream, and getting hold of a line attached to a torpedo, took up the obnoxious article, or the buoy (I am not certain which), at the bow of the boat." He had obviously mistaken Fentress's action aboard the *Marmora* as action aboard the *Cairo*.

44. Ibid., pp. 549, 548; McDaniel-Ewing Claim; Statement of Davis.

45. Dixon Ericson noticed at the *Cairo* exhibit in the Vicksburg National Military Park in September 1991 that there were no cutlasses on display. Many artillery short swords were recovered from the wreck site. When the *Cairo* was commissioned by the army, it was outfitted with artillery short swords in lieu of naval cutlasses for boarding parties.

46. McDaniel-Ewing Claim. Ewing's report is that of a person who sees certain

portions of an event and fills in the missing portions by making what he considers logical conclusions.

47. Sutherland to Ellet, December 12, 1862.

48. *ORN*, Ser. I, vol. 25, p. 551.

49. Microfilm Z707M, Sharkey (H. Clay) Papers, Private Manuscript Collection, MA. Clay Sharkey was a prolific postwar writer. He was born in 1844 although the 1860 Census for Hinds County, Mississippi, p. 581 shows his age as fourteen. In 1862, he was a private in Company C, Third Mississippi Regiment, assigned to Haynes' Bluff, where Higgins's artillery was located. Sharkey wrote at least two pieces regarding his activities in that area as they related to torpedoes ("The First Torpedo," *Our Heritage* [McComb, Mississippi], originally published in August 1915 and reprinted in March 1972, and "Laying a Mine," *Mississippi*, February 1929; copies of both are in the Sharkey Papers). He was apparently detailed as an extra hand to help some of Weldon's crews. Sharkey's stories are hyperbole at best, and the important details of his recollection are in direct conflict with everyone else's recollection (e.g., he says Weldon was "originally" from Virginia; he refers to the *Cairo* as a transport with 1,500 men on board; he says most men on board went down with the ship; the sinking occurred on December 6; he took prisoners of war from the sinking *Cairo*; the Yazoo had a "strong current" at that time, making the handling of the torpedoes hazardous). George C. Osborn, ed., "Notes and Documents: My Confederate History—Clay Sharkey," *Journal of Mississippi History* 4 (October 1942): 228–34, repeats Sharkey's misinformation, adding that Weldon was "born" in Virginia and that the torpedo that blew up the *Cairo* was the "first mine ever known." Sharkey also had an article, "Confederate Floating Mines," in *Confederate Veteran* 23 (April 1915): 167.

50. *ORN*, Ser. I, vol. 25, p. 545.

51. *St. Louis Daily Democrat*, December 19, 1862.

52. Porter made several other errors in that same report. He said the *Signal* and *Marmora* had proceeded thirty miles up the river instead of eighteen miles as those on scene reported and that the ram USS *Lioness* assisted the crew of the *Cairo*, although the *Lioness* was not on the Yazoo at that time. He did not mention the ram *Queen of the West*, which was present. Porter was obviously operating from limited information or was careless about the facts. Porter's letter was published in the *ORN*, but none of the Confederate documents were so researchers who depended on Porter were led astray. See, for example, Virgil Carrington Jones, *The Civil War at Sea* (New York: Holt, Rinehart & Winston, 1961), 2:296, which repeats the information about the *Lioness*. Jones noted (p. 294) that the torpedoes found in the western waters were usually "ordinary demijohns" arranged "to be set off by a pull on a connecting wire attached to friction primers and fastened to objects on shore, or by galvanic batteries controlled by Confederates concealed along the banks." Jones did not say which system was used to sink the *Cairo*. Nash, *Naval History*, p. 155, says the device that sank the *Cairo* was a "demijohn filled with gunpowder and fired by means of a friction primer and a trip wire running from a so-called torpedo pit on shore."

53. R. O. Crowley, "The Confederate Torpedo Service," in Philip Van Doren

Stern, ed., *Secret Missions of the Civil War* (New York: Rand McNally, 1959), pp. 207–12.

54. Isaac Brown to Stephen Mallory, December 25, 1862, from Yazoo City, Mississippi, C225, NA. Brown incorrectly dated the sinking of the *Cairo* as December 14.

55. *ORN*, Ser. I, vol. 25, p. 548.

56. Ibid., p. 549. Although a naval anchor is shown in the drawing, it is highly doubtful that one was used at any time on a torpedo in the Yazoo. The anchor is probably the naval officer artist's license. The statement of Curry and the others reported only that Burton returned with "weights" for use as anchors (C225, NA).

57. A purist could contend that item "D" might be a drawing of a twisted pair of wires instead of a rope. Fentress does describe "D" as a wire but does not describe a twisted pair or insulation.

58. Dual ignition systems are very common in handling explosives, particularly those that are extremely hazardous if they do not explode on the first try or those that must function properly the first time they are used.

59. Isaac N. Brown, "Confederate Torpedoes in the Yazoo," in Robert U. Johnson and Clarence C. Buel, eds., *Battles and Leaders of the Civil War*, 4 vols. (New York: Century, 1887–88), 3:580.

60. McDaniel-Ewing Claim; Milton F. Perry, *Infernal Machines: The Story of Confederate Submarine and Mine Warfare* (Baton Rouge: Louisiana State University Press, 1965), p. 33.

61. Perry, *Infernal Machines*, p. 33.

CHAPTER 3: *We Know She Is at the Bottom*

1. Statement of T. O. Davis, February 25, 1863, C225, NA. I have extrapolated dates in the documents by Davis and Ewing because they did not state the exact dates.

2. McDaniel-Ewing Claim, March 23, 1863, C225, NA.

3. Statement of D. M. Currie, February 10, 1863, ibid. Currie, who uses exact dates, also states that the probe for, and finding, the location of the boat took place on December 15.

4. All these men provided statements for either McDaniel or Weldon during the pendency of the two claims. Each describes his activities for those two or three days, in greater or lesser detail. It is possible that there were other persons present who are not mentioned or did not provide a statement.

5. *Register of Officers of the Confederate States Navy, 1861–1865* (Washington, D.C.: U.S. Government Printing Office, 1931), RG 45, NA. Francis Edgar Shepperd was a native of North Carolina who, before the war, was a lieutenant in the United States Navy, having entered on duty in October 1849. He was commissioned from the United States Naval Academy. He resigned his commission and accepted a commission as a first lieutenant in the Confederate States Navy in July 1861. He commanded the Confederate steamers *Florida* (*Selma*) and *Mobile*. He was assigned to Isaac Brown's command in 1862–63. Following the withdrawal from

Yazoo City, he repaired to Charleston, South Carolina, probably with Brown, and served aboard the *Charleston* and commanded the steamers *Palmetto State* and *Torch* during 1863–64. For the remainder of the war, he commanded the Confederate steamers *Fredericksburg*, *Hampton*, and *Virginia* (No. 2) in the James River Squadron. See also Compiled Service Record of Francis E. Shepperd, RG 109, NA.

6. Statement of Davis.

7. Statement of Charles T. Brooke, February 18, 1863, C225, NA. The statement of Stewart and Johnston is similar in detail to Brooke's. McDaniel-Ewing Claim. Ewing reported that the piece of board recovered bore the title, "Flag Officer Foot Cairo." Edwin C. Bearss, *Hardluck Ironclad*, 2d ed. (Baton Rouge: Louisiana University Press, 1980), p. 150. Bearss, who raised the *Cairo*, reports finding ordnance boxes stenciled: "To Capt. A. H. Foote, Cairo, Ill." The torpedo crew may have found a piece of an ordnance box, several of which were aboard the *Cairo*. Some of the recovered boxes, with their stencils, are on display at the *Cairo* exhibit at the Vicksburg National Military Park.

8. McDaniel to Pettus, December 14, 1862, Administration of Governor John J. Pettus, Correspondence and Papers, vol. 50, RG 27, MA. Currie noted that the wreck was located on December 15.

9. Statement of George Work, July 16, 1863, C225, NA. Work noted that a "water tank" from the *Cairo* was exhibited with "pride and pleasure" by Governor Pettus.

10. Isaac N. Brown to Governor Pettus, December 19, 1862, from Yazoo City, Mississippi, Administration of Governor John J. Pettus, Correspondence and Papers, vol. 50, RG 27, MA.

11. Report of special correspondent Galway, December 17, 1862, "The War in the Southwest: The Destruction of the Gunboat Cairo by a Torpedo in the Yazoo River, etc," *New York Times*, December 25, 1862, p. 2, col. 3. The only purpose of a well-roughened wire in fulminating powder is friction and subsequent ignition.

12. Isaac N. Brown to Secretary of the Navy S. R. Mallory, December 25, 1862, from Yazoo City, Mississippi, C225, NA.

13. This incident demonstrates a now commonly understood military axiom: a mine field or other tactical barrier must be covered by fire to be truly effective as a barrier or channel (David D. Porter, *Naval History of the Civil War* [1886; rpt. Secaucus, N.J.: Castle, 1984], pp. 286–87). The fleet moved through McDaniel's unguarded mine field but could not negotiate both Weldon's raft and mine field under fire and stay stationary to fight Higgins's artillery. When it tried, the *Benton* was cut to pieces and the flotilla forced to retire.

14. Statement of James J. Dees, July 5, 1864, C225, NA. Dees said that he was with McDaniel from October 1862 until "the fifth of January 1863 at which time [McDaniel] left the Yazoo River after which I believe he went to Port Hudson, La to operate upon the Mississippi." In McDaniel to Jefferson Davis, July 18, 1863, ibid., McDaniel says that in January 1863 he went to Port Hudson.

15. Statement of John Beggs, March 23, 1864, ibid. Possibly, when McDaniel decided to leave Port Hudson for Baton Rouge, Brooke, Stewart, Davis, Currie, and Johnston, all of whom were local residents, decided to stay in Mississippi.

Ewing did not make the claim in Richmond until March 1863 so it is possible that he accompanied McDaniel at least to Port Hudson.

16. *ORA*, Ser. I, vol. 15, pp. 921–26; vol. 17, pt. 2, pp. 826–28.

17. McDaniel-Ewing Claim.

18. Hewitt, *Port Hudson*, p. 53.

19. F. Jay Taylor, ed., *Reluctant Rebel: The Secret Diary of Robert Patrick, 1861–1865* (Baton Rouge: Louisiana State University Press, 1959), p. 80. Patrick did not know, or did not disclose, the identity of the Confederate torpedo man.

20. Robert Partin, ed., "Report of a Corporal of the Alabama First Infantry on Talk and Fighting along the Mississippi, 1862–63," *Alabama Historical Quarterly* 20 (1950): 588. The purpose of this tactic was to get the Union naval personnel to attempt to recover the cotton bale and, in doing so, detonate the attached torpedo. The "unusual floating log" device, however, sounds suspiciously like the one described by Ewing in his claim. Mr. Stewart might have been George B. Stewart, who had been with McDaniel on the Yazoo River torpedo crew. Stewart's statement (C225, NA) was notarized on February 14, 1863, in Jackson, Mississippi. See also Lawrence L. Hewitt, *Port Hudson: Confederate Bastion on the Mississippi* (Baton Rouge: Louisiana State University Press, 1987), p. 53.

21. John S. Kendall, "Recollections of a Confederate Officer," *Louisiana Historical Quarterly* 29 (October 1946): 1095, 1110, relates the story of a Captain Pryun, Louisiana National Guards, and a Captain Clark, adjutant of the Fourth Louisiana Regiment, who were on detached duty to make torpedoes at Port Hudson. In mid-May 1863, they attempted to float with a torpedo on a raft toward Union boats below Port Hudson. One of their crew deserted to the Union naval forces and alerted them. The Union forces set fire to a nearby riverbank so they could observe the attempt. Pryun and Clark tied the torpedo to a stump and abandoned it.

22. McDaniel to Davis, July 18, 1863.

23. Clement A. Evans, ed., *Confederate Military History*, 13 vols. (1899; rpt. Secaucus, N.J.: Blue and Gray Press, n.d.), 10:72.

24. McDaniel to Davis, July 18, 1863.

25. Ibid. The torpedoes in Bayou Teche would have slowed the Union gunboats providing cover for the advancing army from the bayou but had no effect on boats in Grand Lake.

26. Ibid.

27. Compiled Service Record, Captain McDaniel's Company, Secret Service, Captain Zedekiah McDaniel, RG 109, NA, contains a voucher signed by McDaniel showing his title as "Officer Commanding Submarine Batteries." The $621 probably was to compensate McDaniel for the loss of his equipment.

28. General Henry Gray to John C. Breckinridge; Office of the Adjutant and Inspector General, Letters Received, 572-M-1865, RG 109, NA.

29. Stewart Sifakis, *Who Was Who in the Civil War* (New York: Facts on File, 1988), p. 262.

30. Hewitt, *Port Hudson*, p. 122. The Sixth and Seventh Illinois Cavalry under Colonel Benjamin Grierson traversed 600 miles of Confederate territory from

Tennessee to Baton Rouge in sixteen days. This feat was later referred to as Grierson's raid. The straight-line distance from Port Hudson to Nashville is approximately 470 miles.

31. Statement of John Beggs, March 23, 1864, C225, NA.

32. McDaniel to Davis, July 18, 1863. The only railroad between Nashville and Murfreesboro was the Nashville and Chattanooga.

33. The railroads adopted a safety signaling device after the Civil War that was placed on tracks ahead of a danger or obstruction. The signaling device was a small explosive charge that exploded when the train ran over it to provide an audible alarm for the engine crew. These devices are called railroad torpedoes.

CHAPTER 4: *Form a Company of Men for Secret Service*

1. Sev. Act of Congress, 1 Sess., p. 51 also an act Prov. Cong., in James M. Matthews, ed., *The Statutes at Large of the Government of the Confederate States of America*, 2 vols. (Richmond: R. S. Smith, 1862–64), pp. 22, 26, 85.

2. Although listed in the McDaniel-Ewing Claim, March 23, 1863, C225, NA, the affidavit of A. Lacy was not located at the National Archives.

3. *ORA*, Ser. I, vol. 22, pt. 2, pp. 973–74, 1017.

4. Answers to Interrogatories of McDaniel, Lieutenant Sydney Hugh McAddam, Confederate States Artillery, April 2, 1863, American Hotel, Richmond, Virginia, C225, NA. McAddam's name is spelled McAdam on occasion in the records.

5. Stephen Mallory to General John Freeman, May 19, 1863, C225, NA.

6. Z. McDaniel to Jefferson Davis, July 18, 1863, at Richmond, Virginia, C225, NA. McDaniel said that "I have never before last week taken the time to repair to Richmond to look after my claim." July 18, 1863, was a Saturday.

7. Secretary of War Seddon to General Freeman, May 19, 1863, at Richmond, C225, NA.

8. Statement of George Work, July 17, 1863, C225, NA.

9. Clark's letter was not found in NA.

10. Bruce to Jefferson Davis, July 20, 1863, with endorsements by Davis and Mallory, C225, NA. See Stewart Sifakis, *Who Was Who in the Civil War* (New York: Facts on File, 1988), p. 36. Horatio Washington Bruce was the congressman from Kentucky's Seventh Congressional District. He was a strong supporter of the war and rarely criticized government leaders. He fled Richmond with Jefferson Davis, left the president's group at Augusta, Georgia, returned to Louisville, and spent the rest of his life in the practice of law, teaching law, and sitting as a judge.

11. Mallory memorandum, August 8, 1863, ibid.

12. McDaniel and Ewing to Congress, n.d., probably late 1863, ibid.

13. Senate of the Confederate States of America, Report of Committee on Naval Affairs on the memorial of Zedekiah McDaniel and Francis M. Ewing, January 6, 1864, ibid.

14. Senate of the Confederate States of America, Senate Resolution 22, January

6, 1864, Joint Resolution for the Benefit of Zedekiah McDaniel of Kentucky, and Francis M. Ewing, of Mississippi, ibid.

15. John Freeman and George Dixon to President Jefferson Davis, April 5, 1864, at Richmond, ibid.

16. Secretary Memminger to President Jefferson Davis, May 21, 1864, Letters Sent, Secretary of the Treasury, 1864, RG 109, NA.

17. Ibid. A chart at the *Cairo* exhibit at the Vicksburg National Military Park shows the value, including changes, materials, and so on, at the time of her construction to be a total of $116,530.

18. Ibid.

19. James D. Richardson, ed., *The Messages and Papers of Jefferson Davis and the Confederacy* (1905; rpt. New York: Chelsea House, 1966), pp. 472–77. Throughout his letter, Davis repeatedly refers to Brown's letter to Mallory of December 25, 1862, describing the sinking of the *Cairo*, the construction of the torpedo, and the credit due everyone, including Weldon and Burton. Brown's letter was included in the claim by McDaniel and Ewing and was apparently the basis for Davis's questioning whether the entire award should go to McDaniel and Ewing. It was an *argumentum ad hominem* to avoid having to deal with the legal issues.

McDaniel in his letter of appeal to Davis of July 18, 1863, wrote that he had paid all of his own expenses from his pocket and received nothing but material support from the government (for detail, see the letter in Appendix). The other persons sent to Johnston and Smith were all enlisted and to be paid the 50 per cent. Apparently, the government was to provide the materials for their operations and the method is not shown to be original patents, but simply destruction of the enemy's material.

20. Ibid., p. 476–77. Although Davis excoriates the Congress, McDaniel, and Ewing for a raid on the treasury, mention of the 50 percent offer appears in many Confederate secret service records.

21. William A. Tidwell with James O. Hall, and David W. Gaddy, *Come Retribution: The Confederate Secret Service and the Assassination of Abraham Lincoln* (Jackson: University Press of Mississippi, 1988), pp. 159, 215–17.

22. Compiled Service Record of Z. McDaniel, RG 109, NA.

23. Confederate War Department, Letters Received, 1863, 906-C-1863, ibid. Carrus's (or Carras's) application was annotated by R. G. H. Kean, chief, Branch of War: "This application is made by Mr. Z. McDaniel who represents this man as one qualified to be very useful in this service."

24. Office of the Secretary of War, CSA, Letters Received, 1863, 816-B-1863, ibid. Boynton later formed his own secret service company under an order from Seddon.

25. Compiled Service Record of A. J. Stevens, RG 109, NA. Stevens enlisted on July 19, 1861, at Washington, Texas. The muster roll for Company E, Fifth Regiment, Texas Volunteers, shows that for the period May–June 1864 Stevens was "detailed by Secretary of War in Trans-Mississippi Department since December 1, 1863." The muster roll for the period July–August 1864 shows that Stevens was "transferred by the War Department to the Secret Service in the Trans-Mississippi

Department." Evidently, McDaniel's early organization included operations in the western theater as well as in the East. Stevens, however, is not shown in McDaniel's list of company members in September 1864.

26. Tidwell, *Come Retribution*, p. 158.

27. Office of the Secretary of War, CSA, Letters Sent, Chapter IX, vol. 16, p. 200, RG 109, NA; also in *ORA*, Ser. IV, vol. 3, p. 177.

28. Thomas Weldon Claim, C225, NA. The first known document reflecting any interest by Weldon in making a claim is a statement from John Beggs, March 23, 1864, ibid.; Weldon to Brown, May 12, 1864, Demopolis, Alabama, ibid. This was probably the source of Davis's comment in item 1 of his refusal letter to Congress. See Richardson, ed., *Messages*, p. 475.

29. Weldon to Brown, May 12, 1864.

30. Brown to Mallory, December 25, 1862, and his endorsement of Weldon's letter to him of May 12, 1864.

31. Isaac Brown, "Confederate Torpedoes in the Yazoo," in Robert O. Johnson and Clarence C. Buel, eds., *Battles and Leaders of the Civil War*, 4 vols. (New York: Century, 1887–88), 3:580.

32. Higgins to Weldon, December 8, 25, 1862, from Snyder's Mills, C225, NA.

33. Statement of Beggs to Weldon, March 23, 1864, from Demopolis, Alabama, ibid.

34. Statement of Edward Blake, March 26, 1864, ibid.

35. Statement of Francis Marion Tucker, May 16, 1864, and statement of David Curry, July 4, 1864, ibid.

36. Statement of James J. Dees, July 5, 1864, ibid.

37. McDaniel to Pettus, June 5, 1862 (telegram), asking Pettus to get all the tin cans he could and have them soldered into the requisite shape (Administration of Governor J. J. Pettus, vol. 55, Telegrams Received, RG 27, MA).

38. Petition of Thomas Weldon to Confederate Congress [1864], C225, NA. The last statement in Weldon's claim is Stancil's dated September 11, 1864. Weldon's submission was some time after that.

39. "Laying a Mine," *Our Heritage*, August 1915, Sharkey (H. Clay) Papers, MA.

40. J. B. Poindexter to Governor Pettus, December 209, 1862, Administration of Governor J. J. Pettus, vol. 50, Correspondence Received, MA.

CHAPTER 5: *There Has Been No Day When We Were Not Operating Somewhere*

1. Daniel B. Lucas, *Memoir of John Yates Beall* (Montreal: John Lovell, 1865), pp. 20–25. See also James D. Horan, *Confederate Agent* (New York: Crown, 1954), pp. 153–65, for further description of Burley and his later operations with John Y. Beall.

2. William A. Tidwell with James O. Hall and David W. Gaddy, *Come Retribution: The Confederate Secret Service and the Assassination of Abraham Lincoln* (Jackson: University Press of Mississippi, 1988), p. 249.

3. *ORA*, Ser. I, vol. 33, p. 232.

4. Ibid., vol. 37, pt. 1, p. 71–72.

5. Ibid., vol. 36, pt. 3, p. 818.

6. *ORA*, Ser. IV, vol. 3, p. 1079.

7. McDaniel to Major William S. Barton, June 20, 1864, Office of the Secretary of War, CSA, Letters Received, 1864, 368-M-1864, RG 109, NA.

8. Ibid.

9. Manuscript 6640, clothbound, RG 109, NA.

10. Manuscript 6638, clothbound, ibid.

11. Compiled Service Record of Z. McDaniel, ibid. See also Francis A. Lord, *Civil War Collector's Encyclopedia* (Secaucus, N.J.: Castle, 1982), p. 173, for a photograph, drawing, and detailed description of a fused 24-pounder "land torpedo," of which several examples exist.

12. McDaniel to Seddon, September 20, 1864, Secretary of War, CSA, Letters Received, 1864, 613-M-1864, RG 109, NA.

13. J. Thomas Sharf, *History of the Confederate States Navy* (1887; rpt. New York: Fairfax Press, 1977), p. 763, shows a drawing of the torpedo but does not give his source. See also Lord, *Civil War Collector's Encyclopedia*, p. 353. On July 11, 1864, William Moon of Richmond received Patent Number 248 from the Confederate Patent Office for a "clock torpedo." Although Maxwell notes that McDaniel "furnished" the equipment used by Maxwell, it is unknown whether the torpedo carried by Maxwell was a Moon invention or something made up by McDaniel.

14. There are two R. Dillards listed in the 1860 Virginia census: Reuben Dillard, Halifax County, p. 821, Halifax Courthouse, and Richard Dillard, Pittsylvania County, p. 526, Danville. Halifax and Pittsylvania counties are adjacent in central southern Virginia at the North Carolina border. McDaniel was originally from Pittsylvania County, and his family was still there during the war. McDaniel had a penchant for employing family members and close friends. Maxwell, however, says that he "engaged" Dillard's services for the expedition. Neither Maxwell nor Dillard is listed by McDaniel as a member of his company in the roster of September 20, 1864, while they were on this mission. The story of the Maxwell-Dillard operation is written in an after-action letter from Maxwell to McDaniel, December 16, 1864, in *ORA*, Ser. I, vol. 42, pt. 1, pp. 954–55.

15. "Investigation of the Explosion at City Point, Virginia, Aug. 9, 1864," E 127, Miscellaneous Records, Envelope 84, RG 94, NA. A board of inquiry was held on August 15, 1864; its results are found in the same records. The City Point affair is one of the most written-about sabotage incidents of the war. See Charles Rice, "Act of Great Daring," *Military History* 6 (August 1989): 8; Ella Rayburn, "Sabotage at City Point," *Civil War Times Illustrated* 22 (April 1983): 28. The explosion was reported in contemporary newspaper articles. See *New York Times*, August 12, 1864, sec. 1, p. 1, and August 13, 1864, sec. 2, p. 5. The second article lists all the killed and wounded known at that time.

16. Bullock to Maury, August 26, 1864, Office of the Adjutant and Inspector General, CSA, Letters Received, 1864, 3972-B-1864, RG 109, NA.

17. Ibid.

18. Breckinridge to Seddon, September 17, 1864, Secretary of War, CSA, Letters

Received, 53-B-1864, ibid. Robert J. Breckinridge had served in the Second Kentucky Mounted Infantry and had been a representative from Kentucky in the Provisional and Regular Confederate Congress from February 1861 to February 1864.

19. McDaniel to Seddon, September 17, 1864, Secretary of War, CSA, Letters Received, 514-M-1864, ibid.

20. Seddon to McDaniel, September 17, 1864, Secretary of War, CSA, Letters Sent, Chapter IX, vol. 19, p. 181, ibid.

21. McDaniel to Seddon, September 20, 1864, Secretary of War, CSA, Letters Received, 613-M-1864, ibid.

22. Joseph C. Frank's exact identity is unknown. The 1860 Kentucky census, p. 162, shows a Joseph Frank in Louisville, Jefferson County.

23. J. N. Amiss's identity is unknown.

24. William H. Berry, born in 1847 in Barren County, Kentucky, was McDaniel's brother-in-law, Elizabeth Berry McDaniel's brother.

25. The annotation "Va (R)" may have designated a member of the Virginia State Reserves. Several of McDaniel's members had formerly been in those units.

26. C. M. Bosker's identity is unknown. His last name may be Bosher.

27. E. W. Breeden was probably E. V. Breeden, who enlisted on November 21, 1863, as a private in Company C, Nineteenth Regiment, Virginia State Militia. He was in Brown's battalion from November 21, 1863, to January 4, 1864. This unit later became the Second Virginia State Reserves.

28. J. Bunch's identity is unknown.

29. G. H. Burnett's identity is unknown.

30. Stephen Burns's identity is unknown.

31. J. R. F. Burroughs was from Lynchburg, Campbell County, Virginia. He enlisted on July 2, 1863, in the Second Virginia State Reserves and served through January 4, 1864, when he was ordered to Camp Lee, Virginia, by the enlistment officer.

32. This was Samuel McCorkle from Lynchburg, Campbell County, Virginia.

33. J. G. Dill was Joseph G. Dill, who was a member of the Nineteenth Regiment, Virginia Militia. He was discharged for unknown reasons on January 20, 1862, under Special Orders 16 (AGO 62 para 17). He had been furnished as a substitute.

34. D. J. Dillahunt was a member of Company C, Alabama State Artillery. His service record shows that on June 8, 1864, he was transferred by Major General Maury to the enrolling officer at Big Stone. This is probably the same man.

35. W. S. Dupree's exact identity is unknown. The 1850 Virginia census shows a W. S. Dupree in Lunenburg County.

36. W. H. Gwice's exact identity is unknown. The Guice family name is known in Warren County, Mississippi. McDaniel had spent considerable time in Vicksburg and Warren County, and it is possible that this man was a contact from that time.

37. B. M. Harris was from Richmond. He enlisted in the Fourth Regiment, Virginia State Reserves.

38. R. D. James was from Richmond. He enlisted as a third corporal in the Fourth Regiment, Virginia State Reserves, in May 1861. He was discharged in 1862 for unknown reasons.

39. James Keelon's identity is unknown.

40. J. K. Keen was probably John Keen enumerated in the 1860 Virginia census, Pittsylvania County, Bachelor's Hall, p. 411.

41. Oliver Kurtley was Oliver W. Kirtley, then aged thirty-nine, of Glasgow, Barren County, Kentucky. A friend of McDaniel's from his Kentucky days, Kirtley is enumerated in the 1860 and 1880 censuses for Barren County. He was married in 1858 to Sarah E. Dickey (Barren County Marriage Records, Book 4, p. 395, File 12, Glasgow, Kentucky).

42. Charles Loneman's identity is unknown.

43. William Leonard's identity is unknown.

44. F. P. McCarty's identity is unknown. An F. M. McCarty is listed in the 1860 Virginia census at Norfolk, Norfolk County, p. 461.

45. G. W. Neville was George W. Nevill, a twenty-three-year-old blacksmith from Barren County, Kentucky, another old friend of McDaniel's. He is enumerated in the 1860, 1870, and 1880 Kentucky censuses.

46. W. H. Parrish enlisted in Company F, Fourth Regiment, Virginia State Reserves in January 1864 at Goochland, Virginia. The 1860 Virginia census enumerates a William H. Parrish living at Caladonia, Gloucester County, p. 903.

47. R. W. Scott's identity is unknown.

48. Elias E. Sinclair's identity is unknown. An Elijah Sinclair was enumerated in Middleburg, Loudon County, Virginia, in the 1860 Census, p. 560.

49. S. M. Williams enlisted in Company D, Fourth Regiment, Virginia State Reserves.

50. McDaniel's roster was appended to his letter to Seddon and may be found on microfilm, NA Microcopy No. 258, Roll No. 75, Cpt. Z. McDaniel's Company, Secret Service.

51. Tidwell, *Come Retribution*, pp. 49–50.

52. Special Orders 257, paragraph 25, October 28, 1864, vol. 211, Adjutant and Inspector General's Office, RG 109, NA.

53. Adjutant and Inspector General, Letters Received, 1519-D-1864, RG 109, NA.

54. Maxwell to McDaniel, with accompanying endorsements, *ORA*, Ser. I, vol. 42, pt. 1, pp. 954–56.

55. Adjutant and Inspector General, Letters Received, 572-M-1865, RG 109, NA.

56. Endorsement of General Raines, ibid.

57. Special Orders Number 73 (1865), Office of the Adjutant and Inspector General, Special Orders, Chapter I, vol. 30, pp. 377, 381, ibid.

58. See particularly Tidwell, *Come Retribution*, p. 3.

59. Maxwell's report to McDaniel is one of the exhibits listed in U.S. War Department, Military Commission, *The Assassination of President Lincoln and the Trial of the Conspirators* (Cincinnati: Moore, Wilstach & Baldwin, 1865), p. 50. Although there may well have been, by legal definition, a conspiracy to assassinate Lincoln, the positive involvement of the Confederate secret services has never

been shown. McDaniel and company are never mentioned except as an example of a Confederate secret service organization.

60. *ORA*, Ser. I, vol. 51, pt. 1, p. 253.

61. Ibid., vol. 46, pt. 3, p. 1250.

Conclusion: Z. McDaniel Was Active in the Destruction of United States Property

1. Maud Carter Clement, *The History of Pittsylvania County, Virginia* (1928; rpt. Baltimore: Regional Publishing Company, 1973), p. 255.

2. It is doubtful that McDaniel knew about the warrant. Family oral history relates that McDaniel thought the Union troops were after him for destroying the *Cairo*. Perhaps he felt that some of the significant amount of documentation he had created on the *Cairo* claim had fallen into enemy hands.

3. Most of the family oral history concerning Zere McDaniel and his exploits was provided to me by Emmy McDaniel Wideman, Marguerite Altman, and Rosa McDaniel Wideman, Zere's granddaughter, all of whom are now deceased, during the 1950s. Additional information was received in an interview in 1977 from Bill McDaniel, Millen, Georgia. They reported that the McDaniel family in Georgia had hidden Zere McDaniel "in the swamps" to keep him from being found by the "Yankees" because he had "blown up a Yankee gunboat." The family did not realize that his fugitive status was occasioned by the City Point matter.

4. 1870 Census, Georgia, Columbia County, City of Thomson, June 21, 1870, p. 40, Dwelling 367, Family 391. Little Zere is enumerated with Samuel McDaniel. His date of birth is given as 1857 and his place of birth as Georgia, an untruth perhaps told out of distrust of government officials.

5. 1870 Census, Kentucky, Allen County, City of Scottsville, June 1870, p. 151, Dwelling 94, Family 94. Elizabeth and Quinlinnia are enumerated with Milton Berry, her father.

6. Marriage Records, Lincoln County, Georgia, Courthouse at Lincolnton, Georgia, p. 92, records the marriage of Zeri [sic] McDaniel and Lulu Hardin on November 6, 1878. Their five children were Rex (1882), Brantz (1885), Frank (1887), Rosa (1889), and Robert (1896).

7. Thomas W. Westerfield, ed., *Kentucky Genealogy and Biography*, 2 vols. (Owensboro, Ky.: Genealogical Reference Company, 1971), 2:72. See also Monroe County, Kentucky, Marriage Records, General Index, Microfilm 997046, Kentucky State Archives, Frankfort, Kentucky.

8. 1880 Census, Kentucky, Monroe County, June 19, 1880, Dwelling 183, Family 185, enumeration of the family of E. R. Hibbit.

9. Z. McDaniel, Compiled Service Record, RG 109, NA.

Bibliography

MANUSCRIPT COLLECTIONS

Kentucky, State of, County of Barren, at Glasgow, Ky. Records of the Barren County Court of Equity and Criminal Matters (now Barren County Circuit Court), in Office of the Clerk of the Barren County Circuit Court, Glasgow, Ky.

Kentucky, State of, County of Allen, at Scottsville, Ky. Records of the Clerk of the Circuit Court, on microfilm in the Allen County Public Library, Scottsville, Ky.

Mississippi, State of, Department of Archives at Jackson. Record Group 9, Confederate Records
  Record Group 27, Governor's Records
  Private Manuscript Collection

Museum of the Confederacy, Richmond, Va. Manuscript Collection

U.S. National Archives and Records Administration, Washington, D.C. Bureau of the Census. Decennial Census of the United States, various years. Microfilm.
  RG 109, Captured Records of the Confederate Government
  RG 45, Vessel Files

NEWSPAPERS

Correspondents. "The Explosion at City Point." *New York Times*, August 12, 13, 1864.

Galway [Special Correspondent]. "The War in the Southwest: The Destruction of the Gunboat Cairo by a Torpedo in the Yazoo River etc." *New York Times*, December 25, 1862.

Louisville Daily Journal, January 25, 1862.

St. Louis Daily Democrat, December 19, 1862.

PUBLISHED MATERIALS

Bearss, Edwin C. *Hardluck Ironclad: The Sinking and Salvage of the Cairo*. 2d ed. Baton Rouge: Louisiana State University Press, 1980.

Beers, Henry Putney. *Guide to the Archives of the Government of the Confederate States of America.* Washington, D.C.: National Archives and Records Service, 1968. (NARS Pub. 68-15).

Beers, Henry Putney, and Kenneth W. Munden. *Guide to the Federal Archives Relating to the Civil War.* Washington, D.C.: National Archives and Records Service, 1962. (NARS Pub. 63-1).

Boatner, Mark M. III. *The Civil War Dictionary.* 1959. Rev. ed. New York: David MacKay, 1988.

Carter, Samuel III. *The Final Fortress: The Campaign for Vicksburg, 1862–1863.* 1980. Reprint. Wilmington, N.C.: Broadfoot Press, 1988.

Clement, Maud Carter. *The History of Pittsylvania County, Virginia.* 1928. Reprint. Baltimore: Regional Publishing Company, 1973.

Davis, Burke. *The Civil War: Strange and Fascinating Facts.* New York: Fairfax Press, 1982.

Davis, Jefferson. *The Rise and Fall of the Confederate Government.* 2 vols. New York: D. Appleton, 1881.

Davis, Tenney L. *The Chemistry of Powder and Explosives.* 1943. Reprint. Hollywood, Calif.: Angriff Press, n.d.

Dowdey, Clifford. *Experiment in Rebellion.* New York: Doubleday, 1946.

Dyer, Frederick H. *A Compendium of the War of the Rebellion.* 3 vols. New York: Thomas Yoseloff, 1959.

Eaton, Clement. *A History of the Southern Confederacy.* New York: Collier Books, 1961.

Encyclopedia Americana. 30 vols. Danbury, Conn.: Grolier, 1985.

Evans, Clement A. ed. *Confederate Military History.* 13 vols. 1899. Reprint. Secaucus, N.J.: Blue and Grey Press, n.d.

Gibbons, Tony. *Warships and Naval Battles of the Civil War.* New York: W. H. Smith, 1989.

Goodspeed Company. *Biographical and Historical Memoirs of Mississippi.* 2 vols. Chicago: Goodspeed Company, 1891.

Grant, Ulysses S. *Personal Memoirs.* 2 vols. New York: Charles L. Webster, 1885.

Grzimek, Bernhard. *Grzimek's Animal Life Encyclopedia.* 13 vols. New York: Van Nostrand Reinhold, 1973.

Hall, James O. "Hunting the Spy Harrison." *Civil War Times Illustrated* 24 (February 1986): 19–25.

Hewitt, Lawrence L. *Port Hudson: Confederate Bastion on the Mississippi.* Baton Rouge: Louisiana State University Press, 1987.

Horan, James D. *Confederate Agent.* New York: Crown, 1954.

Johnson, Allen, and Dumas Malone, eds. *Dictionary of American Biography.* 20 vols. with index. New York: Charles Scribner's Sons, 1928–77.

Johnson, Robert U., and Clarence C. Buel, eds. *Battles and Leaders of the Civil War.* 4 vols. New York: Century, 1887–88.

Jones, Virgil Carrington. *The Civil War at Sea,* Vol. 2: *March 1862–July 1863, The River War.* New York: Holt, Rinehart & Winston, 1961.

Kane, Joseph N. *Famous First Facts.* New York: H. W. Wilson, 1964.

Kendall, John S. "Recollections of a Confederate Officer." *Louisiana Historical Quarterly* 29 (October 1946): 1095–1115.
Lord, Francis A. *Civil War Collector's Encyclopedia.* Secaucus, N.J.: Castle, 1982.
Lucas, Daniel B. *Memoir of John Yates Beall.* Montreal: John Lovell, 1865.
Mahan, Alfred Thayer. *The Gulf and Inland Waters.* New York: Charles Scribner's Sons, 1883.
Manucy, Albert. *Artillery through the Ages.* Washington, D.C.: U.S. Government Printing Office, 1949.
Matthews, James M., ed. *The Statutes at Large of the Government of the Confederate States of America.* 2 vols. Richmond: R. S. Smith, 1862–64.
Maury, Richard L. *A Brief Sketch of the Work of Matthew Fontaine Maury during the War, 1861–1865.* Richmond: Whittet & Shepperson, 1915.
Miller, Francis T., ed. *The Photographic History of the Civil War.* 10 vols. New York: Review of Reviews, 1912.
Moore, Frank, ed. *The Rebellion Record: A Diary of American Events with Documents, Narratives, Illustrative Incidents, Poetry, etc.* 12 vols. New York: G. P. Putnam, 1861-71.
Nash, Howard P. *A Naval History of the Civil War.* Cranbury, N.J.: A. S. Barnes, 1972.
Nonte, George C. *Black Powder Guide.* South Hackensack, N.J.: Shooter's Bible, 1969.
Osborn, George C., ed. "Notes and Documents: My Confederate History—H. Clay Sharkey." *Journal of Mississippi History* 4 (October 1942): 228–34.
Partin, Robert, ed. "Report of a Corporal of the Alabama First Infantry on Talk and Fighting along the Mississippi, 1862–63." *Alabama Historical Quarterly* 20 (Winter 1958): 583–94.
Perry, Milton F. *Infernal Machines: The Story of Confederate Submarine and Mine Warfare.* Baton Rouge: Louisiana State University Press, 1965.
Porter, David D. *Naval History of the Civil War.* 1886. Reprint. Secaucus, N.J.: Castle, 1984.
Rainwater, P. L., ed. "W. A. Montgomery's Record of the Raymond Fencibles." *Journal of Mississippi History* 6 (1944): 113–18.
Rayburn, Ella S. "Sabotage at City Point." *Civil War Times Illustrated* 22 (April 1983): 29–33.
Rice, Charles. "Act of Great Daring". *Military History* 6 (August 1989): 8, 63–66.
Richardson, James D., ed. *A Compilation of the Messages and Papers of the Confederacy.* 1905. Reprint. New York: Chelsea House, 1966.
Scharf, J. Thomas. *History of the Confederate States Navy.* 1887. Reprint. New York: Fairfax Press, 1977.
Sifakis, Stewart. *Who Was Who in the Civil War.* New York: Facts on File, 1988.
Stern, Philip Van Doren, ed. *Secret Missions of the Civil War.* New York: Rand McNally, 1959.
Taylor, F. Jay, ed. *Reluctant Rebel: The Secret Diary of Robert Patrick, 1861–1865.* Baton Rouge: Louisiana State University Press, 1959.
Tidwell, William A., with James O. Hall and David W. Gaddy. *Come Retribution:*

The Confederate Secret Service and the Assassination of Abraham Lincoln. Jackson: University Press of Mississippi, 1988.

U.S. Department of the Army. Field Manual 21-50. *Ranger Training and Ranger Operations*. Washington, D.C.: United States Army, 1962.

______. Graphic Training Aid 5-10-9. *Demolition Card*. Washington, D.C.: United States Army, 1969.

U.S. Department of the Interior. National Park Service. *The Story of a Civil War Gunboat: U.S.S. Cairo*. Washington, D.C.: U.S. Government Printing Office, 1971.

U.S. Department of the Navy. *Special Warfare Training Handbook*. Washington, D.C.: United States Navy, 1974.

______. *The War of the Rebellion: A Compilation of the Official Records of the Union and Confederate Navies*. 30 vols. Washington, D.C.: U.S. Government Printing Office, 1894–1914.

U.S. Office of Strategic Services. *Sabotage and Demolitions Manual*. Reprint. Washington, D.C.: Office of Strategic Services, n.d.

U.S. Senate. *Journal of the Congress of the Confederate States of America, 1861–1865* (Senate Document 234, 58th Cong., 2d sess., Serials 4610–16). Washington, D.C., 1940–5.

U.S. War Department. *Military Law and Precedents*, by William Winthrop. 2d ed. Washington, D.C.: U.S. Government Printing Office, 1920.

______. *The Ordnance Manual for Use by the Officers of the United States Army*. 3d ed. Philadelphia: J. P. Lippincott, 1862.

______. *The War of the Rebellion: A Compilation of the Official Records of the Union and Confederate Armies*. 70 vols. in 128 vols. Washington, D.C.: U.S. Government Printing Office, 1880–1901.

______. Military Commission. *The Assassination of President Lincoln and the Trial of the Conspirators*. Cincinnati: Moore, Wilstach & Baldwin, 1865.

Westerfield, Thomas W., ed. *Kentucky Genealogy and Biography*. 2 vols. Owensboro, Ky.: Genealogical Reference Company, 1971.

Index